CORRIDORS OF FRUSTRATION

CORRIDORS
OF
FRUSTRATION

SIR WILLIAM TEELING
(M.P. for Brighton, 1944-1969)

JOHNSON

LONDON

WILLIAM TEELING © 1970

FIRST PUBLISHED 1970

I.S.B.N. 0 85307 077 6

PRINTED AND MADE BY CLARKE DOBLE & BRENDON LTD.,
OAKFIELD PRESS, PLYMOUTH
FOR JOHNSON PUBLICATIONS LTD.,
11/14 STANHOPE MEWS WEST, LONDON S.W.7

CONTENTS

7

ILLUSTRATIONS

9

10 ILLUSTRATIONS

CHAPTER I

MY START IN POLITICS

I HAVE SPENT a quarter of a century as the Member of Parliament for Brighton—first of all from 1944 to 1950 as joint Member in the old days of two-Member seats with Anthony Marlowe for Brighton and Hove, and then from 1950 to 1969 as the first Member elected for the newly-formed Division of Brighton Pavilion, which is the only constituency in England called after a Royal Palace. I saw the last year and a half of the longest Parliament in British history since the end of the seventeenth century, and virtually since the Long Parliament of Cromwell; I watched it decay. I was there for the new Socialist Parliament of 1945—the first one in British history to have a complete Socialist majority in the Commons; I watched that too decay; and then I sat through what the Socialists now call the "Thirteen Wasted Years". Perhaps they were, but I have seen the next five years even more wasted under the Socialists whose administration is decaying as did Attlee's Government. What will come next?

I fear for a return of a Conservative Government on a negative vote—with no certainty of what it wants and with a disillusioned electorate—which in turn could lead to a dictatorship, not unlike Continental dictatorships, many of which I have seen grow up and declining; or it could lead to chaos. To look on a brighter side, I believe the Conservatives have enough right-wing elements in their midst to snatch from this chaos an initiative which could make little England, now shorn of her imperial strength, but not yet of her instinctive knowledge of how to govern, and her inventive genius, still a great and useful nation.

11

She is also capable of using her historic role of keeping the balance in world power.

It is true that I have held the safe Brighton seat for over 25 years, but let no one imagine that a Southern Irish Roman Catholic just walked into this plum seat, the original centre of the Protestant Alliance and of "Maria Monk", and not so many years back the home of the great High Church movement in the Church of England; and also at one time, the seat with the biggest majority for Conservatives in the whole history of British politics —62,253 in 1931.

I spent the first 17 years of my political career in apprenticeship from 1926 until 1944, knocking on the door of Parliament, having been first adopted for Silvertown, West Ham, in 1926 just after the General Strike. There I fought the 1929 Election against Jack Jones and was the only Conservative in that area not to forfeit his deposit. I was at the time a member of the Bachelors Club and I remember well after the declaration of the poll at Stratford Town Hall, Jack Jones's little speech. He said: "I wish to congratulate Silvertown on turning down the dirtiest fighter I have ever fought; I have fought many a stiff fight before, but never such a big stiff". And then he turned to me on the Town Hall steps and added: "And now you can go back to your filthy Bachelors Club—and I expect that your father is a member too!" The local Press nervously asked me if I wished to have this printed word for word. I said "Yes". It had indeed been a rough General Election, the first after the General Strike and after Neville Chamberlain had cut down on milk and other allowances for the poor. Jack Jones had always been extremely friendly to me in private, but abusive in public; he always stood me a beer and when in return I offered him a drink he asked for a large whisky.

An outspoken Lancastrian, Jack Jones, whose *bon mots* were famous in their day, had started life as a pageboy in the Derby Hotel at Bury in Lancashire. Strangely enough years later I was to be adopted for the then Tory seat of Bury and made the Derby my headquarters—but the War intervened and I moved on to Brighton. Strange again, that when I first put up for Silvertown in 1926 it was Leo Amery who was my chief sponsor at Conservative Central Office. He got me adopted for Silvertown, where I lost by over 23,000, and forty years later I have handed over Brighton to his son, Julian Amery, with a Tory majority which he obtained of 12,982! Not a bad return reward.

I want now to cover all those intervening years, years always in politics international or national. I believe that I am the last Southern Irishman in the Conservative Party in the Commons representing an English or Scottish seat—there were many when I first was elected; as there were also no less than twelve M.P.s who had started life as Americans. To quote but a few, Lady Astor and her sons "Chips" Channon, Lawrence Kimball, Ronnie Tree, Hamilton Kerr. I was also, for length of unbroken service, the senior Roman Catholic M.P. on either side of the House and was often consulted on Catholic problems by the Apostolic Delegation. I was the youngest Conservative Candidate when I was adopted for Silvertown, aged twenty-three, and when the Flapper Vote was introduced shortly afterwards, the ever-go-ahead editor of the *Express*, and later to become a valued friend of mine in the Commons, Beverley Baxter, asked me to write an article on what it felt like to be wooing the flapper vote. This was a mistake. It led to resentment from the young men "walking out" with flappers in the constituency and to a noticeable falling off in membership of the local Junior Imperial League (as the Young Conservatives were then called). I was their first President for Essex since, oddly enough, though in East London, Silvertown was actually within the Essex County boundaries.

What was my background for all those twenty-five years in the Commons and another seventeen years as a candidate?

I was born in 1903. The only child of oldish parents—my mother was forty-two when I was born and my father forty-seven. My mother died when I was fourteen in 1917 and as an only child I continued a rather lonely life, mostly in Ireland, until I went to Oxford in 1921. It was not an uneventful life since Ower, the home I inherited from my mother in Galway in 1917, was burnt down by the I.R.A. in 1920 and my father, as Accountant General at the Four Courts in Dublin, was a sort of assistant to the Lord Chancellors of Ireland, and finally to the last one, Sir John Ross, an ardent Protestant from the North.

On more than one occasion as a boy, I was caught out late at night in Donnybrook on the edge of Dublin and had to walk with a gun in my back and my hands in the air, as the Black and Tans treated me somewhat unceremoniously.

Politics were in my blood, for the Teelings had been famous (according to the Irish State Papers) as amongst the best sheep and cattle stealers in County Meath in the fourteenth century. Later an ancestor was to have the doubtful distinction of murdering the first Protestant Archbishop of Dublin in the time of Henry VIII, and still later one of our family was Chaplain to his cousin, Blessed Oliver Plunkett in Charles II's reign. Our properties were later sequestered because we were anti-William III. An impeccable Irish ancestry, in fact!

After this we moved from Meath to Lisburn in Antrim in the North, where we became well-known linen merchants and rivals to the Milne-Barbours. My great-great-grandfather, Luke Teeling, represented the Catholics of Antrim at the famous Backstairs Parliament in Dublin and he and his eldest son, Charles Hamilton, were arrested in Lisburn; the former was for four years without a trial in the Prison Ship off Carrickfergus Castle, put there by the famous Lord Castlereagh whom he had originally helped get into Parliament as a Liberal. One hundred and fifty years later the late Lord Londonderry (then Robin Castlereagh) M.P. for County Down—proposed me, newly elected for Brighton, for election to the Carlton Club. We had always been good friends since Oxford days.

My great grandfather's younger brother, Bartholemew, could not enter the British Army or Parliament because he was a Roman Catholic and so he drifted towards Wolfe Tone and the Ulster Volunteers and finally went to France to join Napoleon. He entered the French Army and became A.D.C. to General Humbert. Soon the French decided to invade Ireland, landed at Killala and moved through Sligo. Bartholemew naturally went with them and was captured at the Battle of Colooney. Lord Cornwallis, the Lord Lieutenant, refused to consider Teeling as a French Officer but only as a British traitor (whereas being in the French Army, if he had refused to go to Ireland, he would have been shot by the French for refusal to obey orders). He was hanged as a rebel at Arbour Hill, Dublin, in September 1798. I still possess his braces which split in his death agony and the Erin Go Brach ring which he had been given by his fiancée, Lady Lucy FitzGerald, the sister of Lord Edward FitzGerald.

Half a century later, my great uncle Lord O'Hagan was to be the first Roman Catholic Lord Chancellor of Ireland since the Reformation and also the first Catholic Knight of St. Patrick. My family remained Liberals until Lord Hartington broke away and we became Liberal-Unionists, but my mother's family (she was a Burke of Ower, the place which I inherited from her in 1917) were always Tories. They were always hard up, being small landlords, but with just enough land to refuse to do real work, though my grandfather, William Burke, had been a Gold Medallist and brilliant speaker at Trinity College, Dublin. So when I was a boy my mother was determined that I should not waste my life on a small property in the West of Ireland and promptly let it, largely because of the excellent fishing and a good dry fly river, for twenty-one years to Colonel Claude Beddington, a rich English Jew, whose original name had been Moses and who was the owner of Abdulla cigarettes. His wife was socially very well known in Ireland and in London as is still her sister, Lady Nutting, the mother of Anthony Nutting who fell by the wayside politically, at any rate for the time being, at the time of Suez.

After my mother's death the Beddingtons were very good to me, often having me down at Ower, and Guy, the eldest son, trying rather hopelessly to teach me to cast, on the lawn and even on the river. His sister, the last of the family, is today Lady Powerscourt and has written some interesting books, one of which is not too flattering about Ower just before it was burnt down by the I.R.A. My father and I were nearby on Lough Corrib shortly before this happened and we had two ominous graves dug for us—though by whom we did not know. My father decided that it was time to take me out of Ireland, and distant French relations found me a nice old *château* at Cour-Cheverny, near Blois, where young aspiring British diplomats were learning French at the then highly expensive all-in price of £6 6s. a week. I enjoyed it so much that our near neighbours in Dublin, Sir

Lucas and Lady King, the favourite sister, I had always understood, of Lord Northcliffe, Lord Rothermere and all the Harmsworth brothers, were enough impressed to send their rather lanky
son, Cecil Harmsworth King, to join me there to learn French
also.

Alas the house was over-full and as the owner, the Vicomte de
Sèze, explained to me: "There was no bedroom into which to
put Mr. King and so I gave him the best room in my house—
the drawing-room. What more could I have done for him?"
They put a divan just under the window and next morning the
daughter-in-law of the Vicomte, not knowing that Cecil King
was there, jumped in through the window and landed on the
divan and the already disgruntled Cecil thought this was too
much for him; he packed his bags and left and always, I feel,
blamed me more than a little for my bad taste and choice.

Cecil I have known since childhood days, when his parents
lived near me in Ireland. I have often stayed with him and his
mother after the First War at Aboyne in Aberdeenshire for the
shooting or for dances at nearby Dunecht, the Cowdrays' place,
or for the Braemar Gathering and the Highland Games.

I have read what he has said about his mother and I cannot
understand it. I only know of one other person I have ever heard
say that his mother was evil minded; this was old Annie Lady
Cowdray who once told me this in Vancouver of all places where
I took her two grand-daughters to a wrestling match in 1930.

I frankly was very fond of Lady King. She was of course a
practical down-to-earth woman, but she had lost her eldest son
in the War and with the two remaining ones, Bobby and Cecil,
both at Winchester, she was always terrified of losing them on
the journeys backwards and forwards for the holidays to Dublin
by their being torpedoed in the Irish Sea. She would never let
them sail on the same day. Had the two boys gone back in 1918
on the correct day for the return to Winchester all would have
been well; but Bobby was sent either the day before or the day
after the right day and was drowned on the *Leinster*. She never
quite got over this and thought it was her own fault.

When I went to Oxford in 1921 Cecil King was already there.
He was shy and I always thought very introspective. He fell in

1.   The Author age 5 with his Mother.

2. The Author with Queen Mary at Brighton Regency Exhibition, 1946.

love with a daughter of one of the Canons of Christchurch who had had a deeply religious upbringing. They were married in Christ Church Cathedral and I had to go up to London to Moss Bros. to get a morning coat which the bridegroom made quite plain he wished his friends to wear. From this marriage was born Michael King, one of the nicest of the younger generation in Fleet Street I have known. He eventually joined his father on the *Daily Mirror*.

I remember well being with the late Lord Salisbury's Parliamentary Private Secretary, Alan Graham, at luncheon a few years later and we both asked King what was his uncle, Lord Rothermere's real policy as he always seemed to be changing.

"Policy," said Cecil King. "Why, to sell his papers of course, and you can never do that if you stick to one policy too long—that is Beaverbrook's great mistake."

In the latter years Cecil fell in love again, but his first wife did not believe in divorce, being a Canon's daughter and this I am sure embittered him quite a lot. Eventually she divorced him. He never asked me to his new home though I had often stayed with him in between the wars. In recent years I have only been asked to luncheon, by myself, in the *Daily Mirror* building on the top floor. I felt that he wanted to get back to an old state of friendship, but could not and I rather dreaded the meal and the long silences. He was undoubtedly over-worked and over-worried and now seems to be trying out new economic and political plans. As regards his memoirs, I can only register that his mother was in many ways a great woman and one of the kindest I have ever known, but she hated failures and her curt comment to me when I eventually got married at the age of thirty-nine was: "And high time, too."

Oxford in 1921 was at about its most interesting period for any young man. Still up as undergraduates, were many people who had served in the First World War and others who had not finished before the war and had come back.

Some dons wanted to try out new theories and ideas, whilst others made desperate efforts to get back to pre-war days and traditions and on the whole they succeeded. Undergraduates included people such as Anthony Eden, Hore-Belisha, and many

B

older men who had served in the Forces. Those all mingled with my own generation, straight from school most of us, but there were many like myself who had taken nearly a year off after leaving school to travel abroad and learn languages.

I was destined for Magdalen and there the influence of Sir Herbert Warren, one of Oxford's greatest heads of college and most influential snobs, albeit with a very kind heart, was paramount. Sir Herbert had not forgotten that he was responsible for getting George V to send the Prince of Wales to his college before the war. It is true that the late Lord Derby had influenced this choice considerably, since King George looked on the latter as one of his greatest friends and felt that his eldest son, Lord Stanley, who was also going to Magdalen, would make an excellent companion for his own eldest son.

Soon after the war I was present at what we called "A wine and after" in the College. It meant dining in Hall and took place on a Sunday. Then we all adjourned to drink at long tables in our Common Room and sing popular songs. Many old Magdalen men came down from London. This time the Prince of Wales came down and so did an old pre-war Magdalen friend of his, Eric Dunstan, by now quite famous on the B.B.C. as the man with the golden voice. Eric organised the singing that night. Sir Herbert, who of course could not be present at the Common Room function, expected the Prince of Wales to sit at the High Table in Hall with him for dinner. The Prince had no intention of doing this; he was down for an evening of fun, and what made him still more determined was that Dr. Lang, another old Magdalen man, then Archbishop of York and later to be the Prince's fatal enemy as Archbishop of Canterbury at the time of the Abdication, was also dining at High Table. It was felt by the Archbishop as quite a slight that the Prince did not want to join him, and I have often wondered in later years if that seemingly rather harmless episode in 1922 did not lay the seeds for the Archbishop's unforgiving nature to develop his antipathy for the Heir to the Throne.

I do at any rate remember that it was the first time I met Eric Dunstan and we have had a pleasant and unbroken friendship from that day nearly fifty years ago to this day. Eric, living later on the Riviera, had two great friends, Colonel Eric Sawyer and an American, Barry Diarks, who formed a wonderful partnership in building and converting houses on the Riviera and elsewhere which became famous for their character. They helped convert the Duke of Windsor's Mill House outside Paris—yet another link with Eric Dunstan and the former Prince of Wales who became Edward VIII, as well as indeed with Mrs. Simpson, later the Duchess of Windsor and an old friend of theirs. These friends were, I think, much more to the Prince's taste than any chosen by his father.

However, poor Sir Herbert Warren was not to know of all this as he busied himself after the First World War with collecting a College full of people whom he considered suitable to govern the country in the future. To give him his due, he did just as well as Christ Church or Balliol in producing the people who ruled England in the years between the Wars. To name but a few at Magdalen in my days, there was Robert Boothby and John (Evelyn) Strachey, both great friends and oddly enough then, both Conservatives and running a very good Conservative magazine of which I still have several copies, which was, I remember, financed by the Conservative Central Office in London. Strachey later joined Mosley and ended up a Labour Minister. There was also Lord De La Warr, who had been an Able Seaman during the war and was a Socialist; he was to balance out Strachey in the years to come by becoming a Conservative. There was also Wogan Philipps, now the only Communist Peer. Then there was Lord Balniel, later to become Earl of Crawford, and perhaps one of our greatest national authorities on art; the Earl of Scarbrough, a great courtier, the last effective Lord Chamberlain and a strict banner of plays—a job now defunct. To add to this, he became the most prominent Freemason in the Country. In the theatrical world there was Gyles Isham, and Gerald Gardiner, President of the Oxford Union Debating Society and later Labour Lord Chancellor of England, who had the rooms next to mine in my second year at Magdalen. Add Lord Dilhorne (Manningham-Buller), a Conservative Lord Chancellor, and Hylton-Foster, a Conservative who was Speaker of the House of Commons from 1959–1965, together with quite a number of other M.P.s and one can fairly say that Sir Herbert chose well for such a comparatively small College.

When I had my first interview with him, before I had been accepted, knowing that I came from Ireland, he said, very typically : "Do you know Lord Headfort?"

To which I had to reply, feeling I was committing social suicide : "No, sir."

"Oh, never mind," replied Sir Herbert. "I'm sure your father does!"

Later I was to make friends with Prince Chichibu, the brother of the present Emperor of Japan. He also came to Magdalen and Sir Herbert asked him : "Tell me, what does your name mean in Japanese?" The Prince replied, "Son of Heaven." Sir Herbert sighed, "Ah, yes, you will find we have here the sons of many famous people."

Whilst I was a boy and during the war I wanted to be a diplomat, but my father went to discuss this with Sir Francis Bertie, the ex-Ambassador in Paris. It was just after my home in Western Ireland had been burnt down and we and the Beddingtons had decided not to rebuild.

Sir Francis's advice was : "Diplomacy used to be fascinating when it was difficult to communicate with the Foreign Office and Ambassadors could use their own initiative. The development of the telephone and the aeroplane will soon take all this away and you will be at the beck and call of Whitehall no matter how little they know about the subject, the area or the people."

How right he is proving over recent years. He added further : "You will live until you are sixty at the centre of international life and in comparative luxury. Then you will be turned out and, if you have no country home to return to, it will mean life on a fairly small pension in a small house in London—remembering better days."

How little did he realise what would happen under George Brown! Realising that Ower had been burnt down and that I would never have much money of my own, my father persuaded me to give up the idea even before I got to Oxford. His next choice was either the City or a good civil service job with the security of a pension. I said nothing, but that was not my ultimate aim.

After two summers in France, a country wrestling with her post-war problems, and one summer in a defeated and embittered Germany, and some years of Irish agitation, it was politics for me. At Oxford the place was simply saturated with politics; the idealists of the war, the restless youth urged on by Lloyd George's promises, those influenced by Lawrence of Arabia—the young Jews looking to Palestine and, last but not least, the Tory followers of Garvin, the *Morning Post* and the Maxses of the *National Review*.

I naturally gravitated towards these Conservatives, in as much as their Irish supporters, the Southern Irish Unionists, were the only people who had any sympathy for those like myself whose loyalty to the United Kingdom both during the war and especially in the difficult days after it, was being forgotten. I felt little sympathy then for Birkenhead, Churchill, Lloyd George and Austen Chamberlain who seemed to be prepared to throw their country's friends to the wolves—not because of the Irish in Ireland, but because of impractical sentimentalists of Irish origin in the United States who hated England because of what had happened in years gone by—people who now lived well and happily in the U.S.A., but would never dream of returning to settle in an Ireland they considered backward and suffering from a terrible climate.

And so I moved straight away into the political groupings of post-war Oxford. I never took to the Union and only spoke there twice in four years; I hated it. I was far happier in one of the two Tory Clubs then very flourishing in Oxford. Those were the Canning Club and the Chatham Club. Between them in the years I was at Oxford well over 50 per cent of their old members were in the Conservative Cabinets governing the country. Disraeli was responsible for starting these Clubs in the mid-nineteenth century. Neither had a Chairman. They met about eight times a term, always in a different member's sitting-room after dinner and the host took the Chair. Mulled claret was drunk from the Club's silver cups and the host provided other refreshment. The Honorary Secretary was really the centre of each Club and we had a new one each year. There were never more than about twenty members of each Club. The Canning always considered itself the most exclusive; but the Chatham had more old members in the Cabinet. At that time I remember that Lord Curzon, Archbishop Lang and Lord Birkenhead were the outstanding Canningites—whereas Leo Amery, Lord Peel, Lord Bath, Cunliffe-Lister (later Lord Swinton) and Lord Hugh Percy were our old-Chathamites. At every meeting someone read a paper and we discussed it after in detail. Every year we had an Annual Dinner to which we got down such leading lights as we could from London or elsewhere. In alternate years the Secretary of one or the other of the Clubs was responsible for the speakers and for organising the Dinner. It happened that in 1923 I was the Secretary of the Chatham Club and it was my turn to get the guests. Conservatives in London were always courting Oxford (and I suppose Cambridge as well!), in the hopes of finding new blood for Parliament and 1923, as politicians will remember, was an exciting year politically.

I started off well by getting down for an ordinary meeting Lord Chelmsford, the ex-Viceroy of India, to talk about the Chelmsford-Montague reforms. He was an old member of the Chatham, a young relative of his, Gerald Thesiger, now a Judge, was in the Club and he was an old Magdalen man, so Sir Herbert Warren put him up; that saved us money.

Then came the preparations for the big day of the Dinner which was to be June 8th. Nothing daunted, I wrote to the new Prime Minister, Bonar-Law to invite him down. He refused because he did not feel well enough to take on an outside engagement: he was near the end of his days. I then wrote to the Duke of Devonshire, another old member, to Cunliffe-Lister and to one or two others including an unknown quantity called Stanley Baldwin who was just back from America and was Chancellor of the Exchequer. All refused except Stanley Baldwin. When he accepted I was already in the South of France for Easter with Alfred Beit and Peter Colefax. They both commiserated with me, said the dinner would surely be a flop and, worse still, a considerable loss! One must not forget that at that time there were endless prominent people coming down to Oxford. The undergraduates were not only spoilt in their choice of them, but also limited in their expenditure. Baldwin was certainly not a draw, but Sir Herbert Warren had never met him and so he said that he would again open the College Guest Room to him for the night. We had booked the large Masonic Rooms in the High for the Dinner. Then suddenly we heard that Bonar Law was so ill that he had resigned and to everyone's amazement (and my own great excitement), the King sent for Stanley Baldwin. Peter Colefax came rushing round to my rooms and said we were "made"; it was the coup of the century etc.; and even Sir Herbert told George Banks: "I expected Teeling to get angels, but never arch-angels."

But alas, two days later, with the demand for tickets soaring, I received a most horrifying epistle—Stanley Baldwin, now Prime Minister, felt that he had so much to do forming his new Gov-ernment that he could not possibly get away to Oxford and must most regretfully decline. I went round to Sir Herbert almost in tears. He thought for a little time then he remarked: "I hear that Baldwin hates Lloyd George; Lloyd George is coming down next week. I will write to both the Prime Minister and Leo Amery and tell them this and how important I feel it is that the P.M. should get in first; he's due a day or two before, on the 8th."

My first big frustration looked as if it might be overcome; sure enough, there was a telephone message next day to say that the P.M. had changed his mind and would come down accom-panied by Mr. Amery and would make his first speech as Prime Minister, out of Parliament, to the young men of Oxford. Within twenty-four hours I had to start refusing applications and, still worse, the top table became too full for any but the very great, plus the Canning's secretary, Ralph Assheton, (later Lord Clitheroe, M.P. for the City of London and for a time Chairman of the Conservative Party) and myself. Assheton arranged the Canning Club seating and on the great day we both went off together to Oxford Station to meet Stanley Baldwin, Leo Amery and one detective.

We took the Prime Minister straight away to Magdalen and Sir Herbert and Lady Warren gave him tea in their beautiful drawing-room, which was an adjunct to the President's lodgings built over the Cloisters. There were two things worrying the Prime Minister. One was trying to find Lawrence of Arabia which seemed to him an urgent matter; and the other was more a modern trend which he did not like. A wealthy young Northumbrian, by name Hylton-Philipson, had been elected to Parliament at the previous General Election, and had then been unseated—presumably for over-spending during the election; I have forgotten the details. But what upset the Prime Minister was that his wife, Mabel Russell, an actress, had just been adopted by the local Conservatives to take his place. This, S.B. felt, was wrong; she was not, as far as he knew, politically minded and the idea that wives (or widows) of M.P.s should succeed their husbands was naturally new, since women were not yet five years in Parliament, and especially after Lady Astor's initial experiment it did not seem to him a healthy trend.

Only the other day in my own former constituency it was considered an insult by some people that wives should be interviewed with their husbands. The reason seemed to be only whether they would make suitable wives for M.P.s; but it might have comforted them had they thought that they were being interviewed with a view to succeeding their husbands should anything in later years go wrong with these gentlemen.

To revert however to Mr. Baldwin whom I had on my hands for some hours, the Prime Minister asked me if I would take him round the Chapel and the Cloisters as he was particularly anxious to study the brasses and, whilst we were doing this, I asked him what were his plans for the next day and whether I could make any preparations. His reply I have never forgotten : "I am going over to Chequers for the week-end and I want to go cross-country by the slowest train. I love looking out at the countryside and it gives me time to think."

The dinner was packed, the speeches good but not very exciting and Baldwin's naturally was meant to appeal to youth. A few weeks later Malcolm McCorquodale, whom I have always greatly respected for his judgement, said to me at the Christ Church Ball : "All things considered I think you made quite an adequate speech." What he meant by "all things considered" I never knew, but up to then I had never spoken to an audience of more than thirty people and it was, to say the least, an ordeal speaking to some hundreds with many famous people in the audience. Years after Malcolm McCorquodale came to Brighton to speak for me at my wartime by-Election and he was one of the few people I noticed drifting into the Chamber whilst I was making my maiden speech in the Commons. He said I spoke better—but that was twenty-one years later!

During dinner I sat next to Baldwin and I remember well his advice. He thought that politics was now fast becoming a full time profession and anyone who wanted to be a success, should wait a few years and specialise in something first, since once he got in he would not find it easy to learn anything new. He would always only see the side people wanted an M.P. to see. This advice was not taken enough during the coming years, so that by 1931—eight years after this date—we had well over fifty Conservative M.P.s elected who had been at Oxford with me and goodness knows how many others from Cambridge, who knew very little about any subject, being only on an average less than thirty years of age; they would remain in Parliament as a part-time job, helping to rule everybody else, until round about today—except for those turned out in 1935 or 1945. Next morning when I saw him off on his cross-country journey he invited me to keep in touch with him. This I did over the years, both with himself and later with his family who became my best political friends till today.

There were other interesting dinners and debates. I will only mention two. One was a little earlier when the Conservative Party split ominously over support of Lloyd George : and one over Southern Ireland.

At a dinner of the Oxford Carlton Club at the time of the Lloyd George schism we had sitting at the Top Table Lord Birkenhead and Lord Salisbury who were practically not on speaking terms. Birkenhead in his speech kept on referring to Lord Salisbury and turning towards the then holder of the title said : "Of course, I am referring to the *great* Lord Salisbury" (his father the Prime Minister).

We had a very difficult time over the assassination of Field Marshal Sir Henry Wilson, a great Northern Irishman. Feeling ran very high about this at Oxford and there was a debate in the Union—where the then Earl of Longford (whose brother, the present Earl, did not join the Labour Party until 1936) made a very embittered speech about the late Field Marshal and political assassinations generally. After the debate he was dragged from his rooms in Christ Church and thrown into the pond in Tom Quad there—considered a great insult in those days.

I could go on for ages giving the early background to those M.P.s I knew well and who later did well—or badly—in the Commons, but I hope I have given enough background to their upbringing to make people realise what a closed shop at least this part of candidate-fodder was in those days. To talk of the influence of old Etonians or the Old School Tie is perhaps less accurate than to talk of the influence of the great Universities, and perhaps of yet other closed shops such as homosexuality and religion and their influence on choice for office or, at any rate, for M.P.s.

CHAPTER II

GAINING EXPERIENCE

Politics were not the only thing to interest me at Oxford, we had also what some people called "mad groups" and others called "Lost Causes". I was irresistibly drawn towards the latter and no doubt these have added to my frustrations. One was called the White Rose League. It was essentially a House of Stuart organisation. We always spoke of Queen Victoria as the Princess Dowager of Saxe-Coburg since we only recognised the purely hereditary heirs of Charles I as heirs to the British throne, which meant for most of us Prince Rupprecht of Bavaria as the rightful King of England (and Scotland). Some of our more moderate members were prepared to accept George V as our King but only under the title George III. This was because we maintained that Henry IX, i.e. Henry Cardinal of York the Young Pretender's brother, when he died left the remaining Crown Jewels which he possessed to George III and thus, we claimed, handed over to him the Stuart claim. We held an annual dinner and one arch-priest was Dermot Morragh who claimed descent from the last Kings of Leinster and wore, as well as I can remember, a green sash across his evening shirt when presiding at our dinners and spoke in the Royal "We" when carried away with enthusiasm. Later he became a well-known writer on *The Times*, is today in the Herald's Office as Arundel Herald and has recently written a first-class book about the present Prince of Wales. (Has he, I wonder, told him of his secret past?).

Through this strange body I managed to get myself involved in a fascinating adventure. Douglas Lockhart, now a well-known clergyman in Scotland and one of our members, asked me to come to tea one day to meet an Hungarian nobleman called

Count Almassy. The Count had come over to prepare yet another attempt to restore the Austrian Emperor Karl who was then in exile in Madeira. The plan was that a reading party was to go out to Madeira from Oxford, consisting of about a dozen typically British specimens. In our midst was to be one man looking very like the exiled Emperor.

When we got to Madeira we were to substitute this man for the real Emperor who would be feigning illness in bed and we were then to fly back with him to Czechoslovakia. There we were to change into the nearest thing we dared to British uniforms and then cross the border into Hungary. It was calculated that the sight of the seemingly British uniforms would so take the Hungarians aback at the border that they would check with London and that by the time any definite information was received we would already be in Budapest. This was to happen during the forthcoming vacation and the signal for us all to be ready was to be an announcement in the Press that the Emperor was ill. All of us were loyal members of the White Rose League and only one demurred—this was Richard Hope, whose father, James Hope, the late Duke of Norfolk's nephew and later to become Lord Rankeillour, was Deputy Speaker of the House of Commons and as we were sworn to secrecy, the son could not ask his approval and equally felt that he might be endangering his father's position. When we went home for the vacation sure enough we read in the papers of the Emperor's illness. My heart sank a little as it looked as if we were about to start, but the news was only too tragically true and in a few days the Emperor had died.

Things became even more interesting for us after this, because the Monarchists in Hungary were so grateful for our willingness that they invited us out to Vienna and Budapest. It was a most fascinating journey, we were invited everywhere, met the old statesman, Count Apponyi, and also Counts Andrassy and Tisza and others of the Eastern European statesmen, learning all about the problems of Transylvania, Roumania, Slovakia and much that was useful in the years to come. A young Secretary from our legation in Budapest was sent to pump me as to what it was all about—he ended up years later as Sir John Balfour, our Ambassador in Madrid—but he has never told me what he thought of us. Only four of us went out, and we drifted back in different ways, I going to Prague to see Frank Aveling who had been with me and Cecil King at Blois to learn French, and was now successfully in the Diplomatic Corps, but very disapproving of our efforts. I later went on to Dresden with George Edinger. We next started up an Hungarian Review in Oxford to help restore the Hapsburgs. This was my first link with the Hapsburg family which has continued to this day.

Having managed a little later to get a Second Class Honours Degree in History, I moved down from Oxford and at my father's request headed for the City, there to be articled first to Frank Whinney and later to his elder brother Sir Arthur Whinney, the President of the Institute of Chartered Accountants and at the time head of the firm of Whinney, Smith & Whinney. Some of us were articled (at £400 for three years), others were just there at their parents' request to learn business and as we not too seriously hoped, to help the firm in its very large responsibilities.

The two most interesting jobs I had to do whilst with the Chartered Accountants, were to count the cash at the headquarters of the Midland Bank on New Year's Eve and to help do the College audits of Christ Church, All Souls and Balliol at Oxford. For the first I always went round with one of the partners and noticed with interest that the bank kept a special supply of gold sovereigns for Catholic weddings as relic of the fact that the Midland Bank has always had a great Catholic clientèle; when everything was finished I used to go on to the Berkeley to see the New Year in. Gavin Henderson, afterwards Lord Faringdon, was there one year and asked me if I would mind coming round to 18, Arlington Street where his grandfather lived as he expected he would be alone. Sure enough there was the old gentleman, who had made a fortune out of developing the railways of the Argentine and opening up half South America, and who had so many descendants, all by himself standing at the window ready to see the New Year in.

Naturally I was thrilled to get back to Oxford for several weeks to do the College audits. I was amused, if embarrassed, to find the dud cheques of so many of my Christ Church friends who had seemed so opulent when we were undergraduates together.

Christ Church always gave the auditors an extremely good luncheon plus one bottle of excellent port a day, and as I was the only one who drank the port I took my fill each lunch time. As I was only "articled", my fellow accountants let me slip away for a snooze afterwards. We took ten days longer than usual that year over the audit.

When I came back to London Sir Arthur told me that he thought all the adding up and quick transfer work an articled clerk was expected to do was quite silly in my case. My job would one day be that of a big City tycoon and I should know how to preside at Board Meetings, how to help liquidate defunct companies and generally learn to be a City boss rather than a City clerk. He let me sit opposite him in his private office and hear all the telephone calls—several I remember had to deal with the debts of the Wembley Exhibition and others with a tycoon called White who had overstepped himself and who Sir Arthur wanted to continue overstepping himself, so that the City could get rid of that type of person. White next committed suicide and I took the call with the news. Whinney did not seem surprised or worried.

One day he took me to the House of Lords to hear a case being tried. We walked from Old Jewry to the Underground, Sir Arthur imposing in top hat and frock coat leading the way. I was left to buy the tickets to Westminster. In those days we had First Class and Second Class on the Underground. Not thinking, I bought as usual two Second Class tickets. Sir Arthur led us straight into a First Class carriage where he was greeted by another prominent accountant, Mr. Cash and all went well till we reached the Temple. There the ticket collector entered, and Sir Arthur, President of the Institute of Chartered Accountants, was found to be travelling with my Second Class ticket. Sir Arthur was absolutely furious with me and both he and I were sure that by the afternoon it would be all over the City.

The outcome of these pleasant days was that I had not learnt to be quick enough in keeping books or doing the more menial side of an accountant's life and I failed the Intermediate Examination. I felt that I had had enough and so, I think, did Sir Arthur. The net result was that I asked my father to let me try to be a barrister (his own profession so he could not disapprove).

We came to an arrangement with the Whinneys and after a year and a half and no salary—I got £75 back out of my £400— and moved to Lincoln's Inn and a nice flat in Old Square.

I was slowly moving towards my real desire. I had made friends with one of the nicest middle-aged gentlemen I have ever met in London—Colonel H. G. Powell. He was married to a sister of Field Marshal Sir Henry Wilson, as Irish as myself, and their home and family were fast becoming my chief centre of life in London in the evenings. Colonel Powell was head of the Eastern Section of the Conservative Central Office and was steeped in politics. He told me (this was now near the period of the General Strike) how worried our Party were about London and particularly East London. We knew that this area was a hot-bed of Socialism and even Communism, especially down in the Docks, and we felt that it would be a good policy, no matter how hopeless it might seem, to keep organisations working in all the East End constituencies, holding constant meetings, doing endless canvassing and, above all, having healthy-looking young Conservative candidates there, ready to help with their local supporters were there ever to be real trouble.

We may appear, from this distance in time, to have been over anxious. But, after all, it was only just seven years since the revolutions of Europe in 1918 following the Great War, and Russia was becoming daily more worrying : also it was only a year before the General Strike. Colonel Powell told me that anyone who would stand there for the next General Election would not be forgotten later and would get a better seat. I was only twenty-two; it was very tempting, but I had no money, was earning nothing—was living on an allowance of £350 a year and going out to far too many expensive social functions. I remember talking it over with a good friend, J. P. L. Thomas, later to become Chairman of the Party, and the chooser of candidates, First Lord of the Admiralty and a great friend of Prince Philip. He was an even greater friend of Anthony Eden and it was over Eden that our own friendship broke up during the next war.

Jim Thomas said that he felt a bachelor could be an M.P. comfortably on £2,000 a year, but they only then got £400 a year pay and I would be far short of the difference; still my thoughts turned back to Anthony Eden who had been a great if distant figure to me at Oxford. I had then been particularly interested in him, not because I foresaw a great future for him but because I knew that he had his eye on a constituency at Warwick with which he had close connections. His local Chairwoman was a good friend of mine and of my family, Lady Throckmorton, and as Chairwoman, was making it her business locally to raise what money she could. I knew also that Lord Londonderry and Lord Derby and no doubt many other rich landowners, gave money to Conservative Headquarters to help candidates and that they gave it sometimes direct to the candidates themselves.

Well if all this could happen, and Colonel Powell said that he could find the money for me at least to stand and to have an Agent, I argued that I might find my own feet later. I felt I should take this opportunity; and I did. By early 1926 I had got myself approved by Central Office. Mr. Leo Amery had been asked if he could vouch for me as a possibly good Conservative. He wrote back frantically to Colonel Powell to ask a bit more about me—he had only met me for a night in Oxford three years before. Powell evidently did his stuff, I was accepted and then I was sent down to Silvertown (West Ham) to be tried out. Tate & Lyle, the Silvertown Rubber Company (now B.T.R.) with its Chairman as our first Chairman, and Knights Soaps as further backers, all helped to obtain us an Agent and start up an organisation. Later, when the Election got nearer I found that my own Club, the Junior Carlton Club, was putting up the money for my personal expenses and the election, and many of the members came to work for me. But all this was *after* the General Strike and it was only after this that bitterness got real.

During the General Strike I became a Metropolitan Special Constable. I had a "beat" from Hamilton Place, Piccadilly (where was then my old Club, the Bachelors Club, and where I could slip in for port and a couple of biscuits at 11 a.m.) down Piccadilly to Bond Street and up to Grosvenor Square. Nobody ever seemed to break in anywhere and I was made an honorary member of the then fashionable "Chez Victor" Night Club in Grafton Street, where I one night left my truncheon and never recovered it, and of the famous Embassy Club in Bond Street

3. The Author's 21st Birthday Party, Magdalen College, Oxford, 1924.

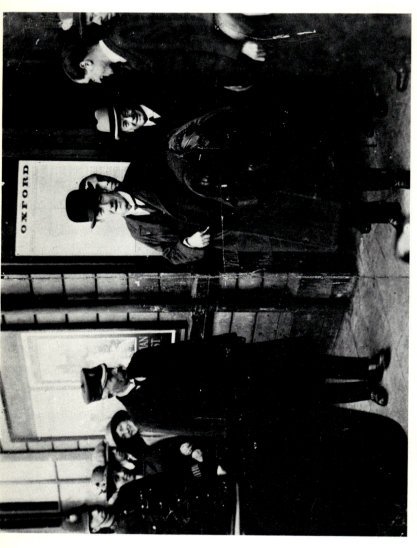

4. Prime Minister (Mr. Stanley Baldwin) and Mr. Leo Amery arriving at Oxford Station 1923, being welcomed by Mr. Ralph Assheton (later Lord Clitheroe) and the Author.

where Luigi let me remain a member from then on. Michael Beaumont, a Conservative M.P. whose son today is Lord Beaumont, the prominent Liberal, was my boss at Marlborough Street Police Station and, since things got more worrying as the Strike went on, he formed a flying squad of police cars and to my horror, I found that I was to be in charge of it. I did not dare tell him that I could not drive. I cannot even now.

Luckily, in Marlborough Street things soon calmed down and the General Strike was over—but not for the miners, who still struggled on.

"Yes," Bob Boothby said to me, "it is over officially, but it will be many a long day before the resentment has died down in the mines."

Baldwin, who had superbly controlled the nation during those difficult days and months, fully realised this and he now turned his energies to bringing peace to the country. Amongst the least easy places was my own area, Canning Town, Tidal Basin, Silvertown and North Woolwich, where I was now about to be adopted at the age of twenty-three.

From the moment one became an adopted candidate one entered, so to speak, the magic circle. That is to say, one was entitled to attend all national political rallies, the Annual Conference where one could hear at regular intervals the Party leaders. As you attended regional conferences, you were put on the list for more political private parties and receptions. This in turn put you in touch with other candidates and you knew a great deal more of what was going on.

From 1926 on, every effort was made to prepare for an election in 1929. We all knew that in our area there was no hope of winning, but it was essential that our viewpoint was put across and that we kept a loyalty to both the Monarchy and the Empire well to the fore.

Our most colourful and probably most intelligent candidate was Anthony Knebworth and to get him or Clydesdale (the Boxing Marquis) who was also a candidate, down to fight in our area was always an achievement. Knebworth had been at Magdalen with me and was always prepared to play, and box. At Magdalen only once was his copybook nearly blotted. The Dean

c

caught him one night very late climbing into College obviously back from a visit to a London night club. To be "sent down" seemed inevitable. But the equally inevitable College President, Sir Herbert Warren, rose once again to the occasion. He declared that: "Lord Knebworth could not have been to London, since he was not in evening clothes"; so our colleague was spared to us.

Alas, Knebworth was killed later flying with his auxiliary squadron and England lost the sort of young man we always needed.

We now formed a group of young candidates for these East End seats—eight of us—and they included Evan Morgan and Johnnie Dodge. Far and away the most active of us all was Evan Morgan who had tremendous courage in taking on the constituency of Limehouse, especially as his father, Lord Tredegar, owned most of the slum property there. He married shortly afterwards a well-known beauty, Lois Sturt, whose brother, Naps Alington, was a fascinating and witty international playboy.

Evan and Lois were married at the Brompton Oratory in real pomp and splendour. Not only did the Mayor of Newport (Mon.) turn up, where most of the Tredegar wealth, in the form of mines—then not nationalised—came from, but so also did the Mayor of Stepney, where much needed doing in the form of re-housing the people. I was an usher at the wedding and had been given the job of collecting first the Archbishop of Cardiff who, in full scarlet robes, was to perform the ceremony.

Another famous character present was the fabulous Rosa Lewis who owned the Cavendish Hotel in Jermyn Street. The moment she saw the Archbishop approach the altar she announced (it was only 11 a.m.) in a loud voice: "Oh, there's the Pope—at last I've seen the Pope."

Ernest Thesiger and Patrick Balfour (later to be the well-known writer Lord Kinross) both hushed her and said: "It's not the Pope."

"Of course it is," she replied. "Evan would never be married by anyone but the Pope."

It said much for the Morgans that they both were immensely popular in Stepney. I wonder, however, if Colonel Johnnie Dodge was not even more of a success next door in Mile End. This was as much due to his mother as anything else. Here really was a dynamic woman, Mrs. Lionel Guest, an American and known to everyone as "Aunt Flora". She fully entered into the spirit of things. She saw the object to be not so much the obtaining of votes, as letting the local people see how the other half of England lived and the why and the wherefore of much that seemed inexplicable and unfair to the inhabitants of the Mile End Road. She got everyone she could to come down and speak to them at non-political tea parties every week.

Funnily enough, Lady Astor when she came was not such a great success since she was dressed very sombrely—whereas Queen Mary's Lady-in-Waiting, Lady Airlie, came almost dressed as a Gainsborough picture and the locals adored it. Soon we were all holding these sort of parties and I managed to rope in a kind and lovely American friend, Olive Lady Greville (the mother of Sir Hamilton Kerr, now the ex-M.P. for Cambridge) to do the same for me. She got together, with her hard-working secretary Miss Daisy Tucker, a number of devoted and good-looking ladies who came down week after week, put on impromptu shows in the Canning Town Town Hall, danced and poured out tea.

I produced a few speakers on non-political subjects, and my Wednesdays were soon known as "Tea-Pot Teeling's Wednesdays". To one of them came the portly, but still very lovely Priscilla Lady Annesley who had become a Socialist. On the way back she asked Miss Tucker: "Tell me about this young man, why does he do all this?" To which Daisy replied: "Because he's the local Conservative Candidate of course and wants to get their votes." "Good God," said Lady Annesley, "and I'm a Socialist."

I did not get the votes; I never thought that I would; but I made a lot of friends and the local women used to say to me, "If only you were Labour, we'd vote for you." Still, when 1931 came and the Socialists were swept from power—one of these seats became Conservative—Mile End where Mrs. Guest and her son had fought so hard. It was won this time by a well-known Catholic doctor who practised at the local London Hospital, Dr. O'Donovan. Our campaigning was well worth it, not only for the Party but for us candidates also and our friends—it showed us a little more of local life, politics and problems which visits to well-endowed Settlements like Dockland and Toynbee Hall did not always do.

This was a five year Parliament, 1924-29, just as long as the present one. Our candidates and their wives today do not seem to have this rather brighter side of canvassing and again nearly all our Ministers' wives, especially Mrs. Baldwin, Mrs. Neville Chamberlain and Lady Worthington Evans, in those days invited us (and our wives if we had them) frequently to their houses where you met each other and the Ministers who dropped in invariably and we were allowed to bring two or three of our own local hard-working supporters and that was the most important thing of all—it meant an awful lot to them. Are there not enough funds in the Party today to help our Shadow Cabinet Ministers wives, or even Ted Heath himself, to throw a few of such parties, and not always at Westminster not so much for M.P.s and their wives, but for candidates, their wives and their local supporters? It would break a lot of the monotony of five years waiting. I hear criticisms along these lines all the time.

On the more direct political line I was trying to press for a new Victoria Dock Road and we had many meetings to discuss it. After the 1926 Strike it became awfully difficult to get any Minister to come to Canning Town or my docks, but Wilfred Ashley (later Lord Mount Temple), our Transport Minister, came and I was naturally grateful to him.

I got plenty of younger M.P.s, such as Ewan Wallace, Tini Cazalet and Terence O'Connor, and one or two older members like Sir Paddy Hannon, but they were all pretty roughly treated and I think hated it. The only one who got it across was little Captain Dixie, the Member for Penrith and Cockermouth, who had the same problems! I became hardened to it all and learnt to speak much better since at Canning Town they put a shell-shocked man in the third row every time I spoke and after three minutes he had the place in such an uproar that I was able to carry on and say what I liked since no one could hear me. I also became hardened in another place, since whenever I went canvassing small children were sent to walk behind me and stick pins in my posterior. When it came to speaking from a rostrum at street corners the Police always stayed on the outside where they could never have reached me if there had been trouble, and then I got the hat pins.

Toby O'Brien, later to be such a famous Public Relations expert, Peter Stewart and Nora Stewart-Brown all came to help me from a Press angle and a Double Blue, Christopher Mackintosh and his tougher friends, formed a "chucker-out group" for my meetings. It certainly was a tough fight at the 1929 Election, but as I said in my first Chapter, I did not forfeit my deposit and I gained great experience for later on.

CHAPTER III

THE SLUMP AND AFTER

T HE RESULTS of the 1929 General Election naturally led to quite a lot of post-mortems in the constituencies as well as at Headquarters. The fact that Labour was to be in power with only an artificial majority—in power officially for the second time, made many people feel that it was not too bad a thing that the Socialists should learn bit by bit how to control a Government and how to run the country. After all, there always was the Civil Service to put a brake on anything too ridiculous. But few Conservative politicians agreed with this and the Committee which chose the posters and slogans for the Election were, I think with reason, much criticised.

"Safety First" was one slogan particularly disliked—it in no way appealed to the adventure of youth and the new electors, but it was thought erroneously that it would especially appeal to women voters. Oddly enough, I was told by Francis Blundell, M.P. for Ormskirk and the Chairman of the group who selected it, that it was the perfect likeness of Stanley Baldwin in the picture which so appealed to them. They did not pay much attention to the caption "Safety First". It did, however, epitomise the man and his Cabinet from 1924 to his retirement in 1936 : and became their political catchword.

During those years between the wars, Britain and her Dominions had to make good the loss of well over one million young men. Those who should have been coming after Baldwin and his friends in the twenties and thirties had been decimated and we were left with much younger men with less knowledge of the outside world. It was essential to lead a restless, at first slightly bitter, and later very bitter generation both in Parliament and amongst the electors, quietly and playing safe. There is little doubt that the upheavals of the General Strike and the Abdication, in other hands than Baldwin's, would have led to much more worrying results. But Baldwin did not have a very inspiring team to work with—Inskip, Worthington-Evans, Lord Peel, Lord Derby, Joynson-Hicks—they were adequate but not brilliant and who remembers them now, thirty years after? Yet Churchill, Amery, the two Chamberlains, Birkenhead, were always in the wings.

Baldwin was a great House of Commons man and went constantly into the Smoking Room where he got to know his fellow Members better than any other Prime Minister. You practically never see Wilson in the Smoking Room now.

I remember well Charles, Lord Londonderry, telling me when I was stationed in Northern Ireland during the war and used to spend many week-ends with him and what remained there of his family at Mount Stewart:

"I was never brought up to think quickly or to argue fiercely and so I was handicapped and shot down in the Cabinet. Yet I noted down my views and in the end I found that I usually had been right in my instincts and decisions; but it was then too late. I just could not get my point across against self-made men and quick-witted lawyers like Robert Horne or Sir Kingsley Wood."

Later on, his son, Robin Castlereagh, M.P. for County Down, told me that when the country or the Party was being split on some subject he could not grasp, he used to listen to the brilliant people at his father's table over the port, and decide to support the majority view. Perhaps the approach of father and son were better for England than those of many people in control now. Robin Castlereagh stood in 1929 for Darlington and, just as I got a fine collection of hat-pins stuck into me and of stink bombs at my meetings, so did he—only worse; one hat-pin pierced his lung.

Not only were the elders of the Party unhappy about what had happened in 1929, but so were we younger candidates; we felt we were scarcely ever consulted and we decided to form ourselves into a Candidates' Dining Club, all being determined to fight another fight. Lord Curzon (later Earl Howe), the great racing motorist, was then a Whip and he was detailed to keep in touch with us. Hugh Molson was our Treasurer and I was Secretary. Thelma Cazalet, Irene Ward and John Mellor were all active members. Everyone became an M.P. except myself, two years later in 1931, but many were out again in 1935 and still more in 1945.

Why did I not continue? Actually I did until the summer of 1930. I looked round for a safe seat, as did we all, and I was chosen fairly soon for another Labour-held Essex seat, East Ham North, with fair chances of winning it. The sitting Member was then a quite famous well-to-do Socialist, Miss Susan Lawrence. My successor defeated her in 1931 easily but the seat soon reverted to the Labour Party. My experiences at Silvertown and then returning as a contrast to the dinners and ballrooms of West London night after night, much though I enjoyed them, left me uneasy. The Bright Young Things were very much to the fore; I knew them all and we used to meet a lot in the Café Royal. My two clubs were in themselves different, the Junior Carlton was full of members of the Coningsby Club, enthusiastic Tories but not very knowledgeable about the outside world; more and more I began to feel that I should have more first-hand experience of our Colonies and Dominions if possible, before going into Parliament. But how? The Bachelors Club was non-political and much more snobbish—to have become a member in the days when the old Mr. Gillette—a Beau Nash of the first quarter of the nineteen hundreds—controlled this Club which he had founded was considered something to boast about, as I naturally did; and there were many travelled younger members in it.

A year or so before the 1929 Election, Cardinal Bourne, then Archbishop of Westminster and a good friend sent for me to tell me of a new move in the world of migration. It seemed that the Government aided by the Canadian Pacific Railway, the Canadian National Railway, the Hudson Bay Company, Cunard and the P. & O. for Australia, were interesting themselves in populating vast areas with British born people, and also in getting unemployed people away from the U.K. Indirectly, of course, they were collecting business for themselves.

The Government could not help transport companies directly,

but they could and would go fifty-fifty with recognised charitable and religious bodies in any money these could find to help migration. Particularly wanted were large families. These the Catholics could usually find. They might well be of Irish origin in Liverpool or Glasgow or London, but that did not matter. The Cardinal too thought it a good idea, but he wanted to be sure that these people would not be lost to the Church on leaving the U.K. or Northern Ireland (which was included in the grants). He proposed starting up the Catholic Emigration Society and he wished me to be its first Chairman. I was then twenty-five.

It would have a paid staff and an influential Committee and the Government side would be represented by Lord Lovat, himself a very go-ahead Catholic who had formed the Lovat Scouts and who had had a deep attachment to my uncle when he was teaching near his home many years before at Fort Augustus. There was, however, no pay in it for me and I was beginning to realise that a small allowance and an occasional gamble on the Stock Exchange could not keep me much longer. But this fascinating job and the coming General Election would keep me pretty tied. At the other end the C.P.R. and the C.N.R. were paying for a Catholic Reception Committee in Canada and it did look as if I might one day get out to Canada as the Railways' guest for a bit; an opportunity to travel. So I accepted.

In 1930 Lord Beaverbrook became more and more prominent in promoting his Empire Crusade in the *Daily Express* and I must say that I became more and more interested. Next door to me in East Ham South was now standing Hubert Duggan, the stepson of Lord Curzon of Kedleston. I saw a good deal of him and heard still more about the Argentine from where, in only two generations, his family from a poor Irish background had built up a huge fortune.

Hubert Duggan was later adopted for Acton and he in turn was succeeded as M.P. by Henry Longhurst whom I have always looked on as the nicest of Golfing Correspondents and who I wished had continued his parliamentary career. Henry made his maiden speech the same day as I did. At the end of the debate it is customary for the Front Bench speaker to refer to maiden speeches. Eden referred flatteringly to his but there was no men-

tion of mine—where I had criticised Foreign Policy, until Tom
Driberg intervened and asked : "What about the maiden speech
of the hon. and gallant member for Brighton?" Eden then had
to refer to it. Harold Nicolson, then writing a column in *The
Spectator*, did not miss this—so I had early on a black mark
from Eden.

Lady Curzon in early 1930 decided to give a big reception at
Carlton House Terrace for her son's leading constituents, and
Mrs. Baldwin was to help her receive the guests; almost everyone
accepted. Then suddenly Conservative Headquarters advised that
this would be bribery and the only way to hold the party was to
charge a guinea for every ticket. Those who had accepted could
hardly now refuse and many were furious at seemingly being
trapped; but the party was a huge success. Tini Cazalet and
myself acted as sort of introducers, making sure that everyone
got to know the more important guests. I saw one rather nice
young man looking lonely and went over to speak to him : "I
suppose you are a member of the Junior Imperial League," said
I. "No," he replied, "I am a detective."

There were several Essex M.P.s at that party and it was with
Essex M.P.s that I was to quarrel, especially the Ilford one, Sir
George Hamilton. To my mind Lord Beaverbrook was giving the
public something that they wanted, a larger horizon and a feeling that Britain had a future with her Empire—we must try it
out. I took my courage in my hands and wrote to ask Lord
Beaverbrook if he would come to East Ham and impart his
message to my supporters. He accepted and I took the Town
Hall. I expected opposition from the official Conservative Party
in Essex, but not at all; I found instead that the Conservative
M.P.s merely complained that Beaverbrook was coming to me,
a mere candidate, whereas he should come to them, prominent
M.P.s, to speak for instance in more central Ilford Town Hall.
In the end, thanks to Colonel Powell of Central Office, I won
the day and we had over 2,000 people in the East Ham Town
Hall with music laid on by the Empire Crusaders to play, "Here
the Conquering Hero Comes" as Lord Beaverbrook walked to the
platform, and well he deserved it. It was a dynamic speech by a
dynamic friend of this country. I chose mainly local candidates

to be on the platform but thought it would be a nice gesture to invite Ian Campbell, his son-in-law (later Duke of Argyll) to come on the platform too.

It meant coming from the Riviera where he was engaged in fruit farming and his father-in-law did not approve at all. We were also held up nearly a quarter of an hour for Sir Gifford Fox, the future M.P. for Henley, whose father had been a great friend of Beaverbrook. His excuse, however, could not be frowned upon; his wife gave birth to (what proved later their only child) a daughter that evening. She is one of the few women whose age I have no trouble in guessing.

It is now difficult to imagine what a stir Lord Beaverbrook's campaign had in the Conservative Party—it laid the foundation for the Ottawa Agreements—and what he said that evening made my mind up to accept the invitation of the Canadian Railways and Cunard to spend a year in Canada, to see for myself the work of migration bodies and what were their possibilities.

Today many would not even realise what was this Empire Crusade which Lord Beaverbrook started. Very briefly, in those days from 1929 until the Ottawa Agreements, England was deeply depressed by unemployment.

Lord Beaverbrook, with his intimate knowledge of Canada and his love for the British Empire, came forward literally to start a Crusade to make the Empire realise its might and its potentialities, in fact to pull itself together. He was an inspiring speaker and it struck a chord up and down Britain. Canada, Australia, New Zealand, South Africa, the West Indies, why could we not build a tariff wall around them and get especially our food from them? They in turn would take our factory production. He was, I still think, right. Even now with adjustments much of it could be achieved. Most of us would prefer it to uniting with Europe—but there is no one today appearing to carry the torch as he did. Even though it was never completely attempted—we did well a few years later in getting the Ottawa Agreements which brought certain preferences to Empire goods and I believe that, as in many other things, Britain owes Lord Beaverbrook an irreparable debt. What a dynamic fighter he was!

The railways were to give me free passes as did Cunard; the rest I had to find for myself. It also, of course, meant giving up East Ham, and my immediate opportunity of getting into Parliament. I remember going to collect letters of introduction from Mrs. Neville Chamberlain on the Terrace at the House of Commons. Her advice was: "You go at once because you will be wanted back for an election in a year or so. You are now nearly twenty-eight, don't leave getting into the House too late. You should be in by the time you are thirty. That leaves you time to become a P.P.S. before moving into smaller Government jobs."

That was the school of thought in those days. One must spend most of one's life in the Commons; perhaps she was speaking with feeling, because her husband had taken the line which Baldwin was pressing on me—namely to specialise in something outside Parliament before coming in—Chamberlain had first been a great Lord Mayor of Birmingham.

I set sail in August 1930 with an old friend from Magdalen, Cecil Latta, and there never was a more considerate travelling companion. It was the beginning of travel adventures which were to take me right up to 1939. I felt as the years went by that I was learning more and more about the leaders and future leaders of other countries and about their problems and that I could make the greatest use of this information in the Commons later, whereas my friends might all be in Parliament but not have seen at first hand the countries they wanted to influence. As events proved, the war had started before I got to Westminster; and most of what I had learnt was wasted except in writing and lecturing.

One of my letters from Mrs. Chamberlain was to Mr. (later Lord) Bennett who ousted Mr. Mackenzie King and became Prime Minister whilst we were still on the Atlantic. I went straight to Ottawa and presented my letter. Next day Bennett's secretary rang me and said: "The Prime Minister would like you to lunch with him today at the Rideau Club." This again happened the next day and a third time. He was asking me all the time about the political situation in London. I was feeling that I was indeed a success, but his Secretary put me right quickly, "The reason the Prime Minister is asking you out so much is that he is forming his Cabinet. If he is seen with any well-known Canadian, rumours will get around. But he is safe with you as nobody knows who you are."

Anyway, Bennett opened the book of Canada to me and gave me good letters to Pat Burnes and his own partner Nolan in Calgary and made things generally much easier for me. His defeated rival, Mackenzie King, however was unapproachable and I felt despondent at this. I happened to mention it to Lady Willingdon the Governor-General's wife and she promptly replied: "We are going to an Ice Hockey match tonight. Come and dine first and then come back for supper afterwards. I will have him here for you." And she did.

To her also and the Governor-General I owe much of my happiness in Canada. Their son "Nigs" Willingdon later became the most popular President of my Brighton Association I ever had and his wife quite the most beloved. I have written a book about this Canadian visit which in the end lasted nearly a year. *England's French Dominion* was my first book: my theme was that the French Canadians would one day get control of Canada. I cannot claim that I foresaw what is happening now and Lord Beaverbrook disagreed violently with much that I suggested, but first approaching things from the Roman Catholic angle my argument was that the French Canadians resented the migration from the United Kingdom and from Ireland of our Catholics—and Canadian Catholics should in their view be as far as possible of French origin. Nor did they want Central European Catholics coming to Winnipeg and Central Canada. The people of Quebec would continue to breed large families and then subsidise them to migrate to the West. In those days when you had got a certain number of people (a majority) in any one area, that secured a new Parliamentary seat. Thus, bit by bit, the French would get a preponderance of seats in the Federal Parliament in Ottawa and in State Parliaments as well.

It all seemed very far fetched in those days, especially with the increasing pressure from the United States. But is it quite so far fetched today? At that time the French Canadian Catholic Hierarchy was much against too much fraternisation with atheist France—but things are different now and De Gaulle's visit to Montreal and Quebec in 1968 showed up that there is a special department these days in the Quai d'Orsay working all out to make as many French Canadians as possible feel that France is their second home. Canada sent a French Canadian to London for the Commonwealth Conference in 1969. I may have been forty years too soon and there may be great racial struggles ahead; but I feel that Canada is getting nearer to France today than to Great Britain.

I had a free Pass across Canada until 31 December 1930; I used it to the full. I got to Vancouver by September, back to Montreal by November and reached Vancouver again on New Year's Eve. I think that I had seen every side of Canadian life from the naked Doukhobors in Calgary being made to put on their clothes again by the Police douching them with itch-powder, to the timber workers in Northern Ontario in mid-winter. From every Government House and Premier's Office from Quebec to Vancouver; British immigrants from wealthy peers' sons working on Lord Rodney's ranch in Alberta, to our own Catholic settlements in Red Deer and other parts of Alberta. I loved it all and I wanted to go further afield. Political friends, already in the House, wrote from England : "Come back or you will be too late." In Vancouver I got a message that the girl I had hoped to marry had married someone else : and, on receipt of this, I decided to continue into the United States.

I took a boat from Vancouver to Los Angeles and spent some weeks in Hollywood. My only personal letter of introduction to anyone in the U.S.A. was from George Grossmith the actor, a cousin of the girl I wanted to marry, to P. G. Wodehouse in Hollywood. Wodehouse was delighted to welcome me since he pointed out that he had been a year in Hollywood, paid a high salary, but so far had not been called in or asked to do much work and he was feeling neglected. He was hurt when the first anniversary of his arrival had come and the Company had not thrown a celebration party.

I soon learnt that big film companies worked that way—one side organised the publicity and the other got on with the work. P. G. had been chosen by the publicity people as highly suitable to have on their pay role as one of their writers. They never consulted the actual producers and possibly never even told them who they had engaged. It was all very pleasant and there I first met Dudley Delavigne and Tony Bushel, as well as Maureen O'Sullivan who became a good friend; so did her eventual husband John Farrow and to this day I have kept the invitation to their wedding. They have produced Mia Farrow. They were good Catholics and I helped them a bit later on, to get their son into the Oratory School near Reading where I myself had been educated. The Wodehouse daughter Leonora remained a good corresponding friend wherever she was, until the day of her very premature death; she married Peter Cazalet the trainer and brother of two M.P.s, Thelma and Victor. I remembered her mock indignation when she saw the fat cheque P.G. got at the birth of her child, for writing an article on "What it feels like to be a grandfather". He was not her father, only her adopted father.

From Hollywood I moved north via Reno and California to Portland, Oregon, Seattle and across to the Montana State University at Missoula. I then jumped freight trains to Yellowstone Park, hitch-hiked on to Jackson's Hole in lovely Wyoming, joined a Mormon selling vegetables down to Salt Lake City, later moved on to Las Vegas, Nevada, hitch-hiked across the Middle West and the "Bible Belt" to Chicago, stayed with friends (newly made) there and in Philadelphia, New York, Washington, Southern Pines, North Carolina, and eventually reached New Orleans in 1932 just in time to be the only white guest at the annual Negress Debutante Ball held at the time of Mardi Gras.

The world being small, I found that our Consul General in New Orleans had been previously in Bordeaux where I had often met him at my aunt's home and he arranged for me to return on an Italian freight boat to Genoa via Galveston and Houston. These were Prohibition days but he had introductions to a reliable bootlegger. The latter was already in prison for his activities—but he still had a private telephone line to his cell from where he did business. I reached Italy in May 1932 to find a letter from Leonora Wodehouse to tell me that the friend I had been so fond of had just died in childbirth. I went on to Taormina in Sicily to write a book on my year's adventures in the U.S.A. A part of my life had come to an end and what should I do next?

Had I wasted my time and thrown away my political chances? To those defeated candidates in my Party who today are without a seat I emphatically say "No"—if they are young enough—but I did not feel certain then myself. I had seen the America that not every British candidate has seen and it was to stand me in good stead, especially during the coming war.

I had got to realise that, though I never considered myself a foreigner in America, the Americans quite definitely did. We in the U.K. are brought up to think that there is a "special relationship" between us—but we never meet those of German, Italian, Polish Ukrainian, and even French descent plus the Negroes, and forget that they form the larger part of the U.S.A. and know next to nothing about us. The only thing we have in common is our language and, as Bismarck once said, that was Britain's greatest capital asset. At one moment during the war, just after Dunkirk, it was perhaps our only asset and lucky we were to have Winston Churchill, himself half an American, to exploit it, especially on the radio—not functioning in the days of Bismarck! A few years later another half-American and a superb speaker was to be our Prime Minister for a long and helpful time, Harold Macmillan, and it could be that soon we will have another in Quintin Hogg, whose mother, the late Lady Hailsham, also came from the U.S.A. Are there no Socialists with American mothers?

Most of my political friends had been defeated in 1929 but all were in in 1931. Early in 1931, they began to drop off telling me to return as every decent seat seemed filled and I myself was fascinated, watching the U.S.A. struggling to get back from the slump and still quite determined not to have unemployment relief—which they wrongly and contemptuously called the dole.

When September 1931 came with the General Election I was just heading for Salt Lake City, the heart of the Mormon country, where there were then in the area well over one million Mormons; at least a quarter of them were by origin British. Mormonism seems to have a particular fascination for the British, as being very Nonconformist and capitalistic. At that time Senator Smoot, a prominent Utah Mormon, was Chairman of the Senate Finance Committee, one of the most influential posts in U.S.A. politics. He was in Salt Lake City when our finances collapsed

in September 1931 and we went off the Gold Standard. I saw
him several times then and he was deeply interesting.

"Never," he told me, "would the U.S.A. let Britain really
collapse." But he felt that we had so overspent ourselves that
credit was nowhere obtainable and he took a particularly dim
view of what he considered our moral deterioration due to the
dole and the general feeling of unwillingness to work. I instinc-
tively felt that this was only half true, but I had no proofs. I was
to obtain them when I got home and visited our unemployed.
He sent me to speak to a rally of British Mormons—over 600 of
them—who were assembled in a big hall, grouped under banners—Cardiff, Birmingham, Newcastle and so on. There were
ex-members of the Junior Imperial League, who had just recently
come out and assured me that reports were exaggerated.

What I did know was that my allowance was now effectively
cut in value by the 1931 devaluation and, as I was also pretty
short of introductions across from Utah until I got to Chicago,
I would do well to send my luggage on and take to the road to
see what friends I might make and what and who I might get
to know. I travelled *via* Colorado, Kansas and Idaho and it was
a great success. Few people gave me lifts for more than twenty
or thirty miles and most of them were more than willing to tell
me their success stories. The best tip I got, going through the
Bible Belt, was: "Study the Bible, it pays hands down."

I've watched the truth of that advice in Moral Rearmament,
Aimee Semple MacPherson, Hot Gospellers, and many others.
But I will always remember that the Mormons in the West
were, and I believe still are, our greatest friends. They have
now built their temple at Lingfield in Surrey and I hope that
they are doing well there. Incidentally, Enoch Powell may be
interested to know that no Negro is accepted as a Mormon; the
Mormons consider the Negroes to be the decendants of Cain.

I shall never forget the dislike, if not terror, felt in many parts
of the U.S.A. for the Negroes. The Negro may not yet be our
chief problem in the U.K.; but he certainly is fast becoming the
great worry of the U.S.A., both in the North and in the South.

Again we must remember—and this became very apparent
after the war—bit by bit, more and more better-off people are

D

moving from the East of the U.S.A. to the West and this area is therefore becoming more and more the Conservative area. If we take a look at the map we will also see that for the West of the U.S.A., China, Japan and the Far East are much nearer than is Europe or the Russian Communist menace.

The Westerners are not only looking to a future trade with that part of the world, but are conscious of what Japan did in 1942/43 and what China could well do in the near future. There is nothing but sea, except Formosa, between most of the Chinese coast and the Californian coast—but there is all Africa and Europe between New York or Chicago and the U.S.S.R. Lastly, let us not forget that there is a far larger number of people in the U.S.A. of Irish origin than there are in Ireland. Not all these are from the South, there is a strong Ulster contingent, but Ireland's problems and her differences with Britain will always be of interest to this large section of Americans.

On leaving America and whilst in Sicily I was in touch with *The Times*. This came about through an old Magdalen friend, the Earl of Iddesleigh. I had been his Best Man when he married the daughter of the famous writer Mrs. Belloc Lowndes—Hilaire Belloc's sister. He knew all about my Canadian and American tour since he succeeded me as Chairman of the Catholic Emigration Society. Lady Iddesleigh's father, Mr. Lowndes, was also the Obituary Editor of *The Times*. Between them they told Mr. Barrington Ward, the Editor, of my hitch-hiking experiences in the U.S.A. and he asked me to write some "Turnovers" as they were called, on this. The Turnover used to be the last column on the right hand side of the centre page and usually turned over on to the next page. I sat down laboriously to write these but, when I submitted them, the Editor sent for me and said : "We have got our well-paid expert correspondents in the U.S.A. and throughout the world, they can do all this. What we want from you is the real day to day experience with as few figures and generalisations as possible." I went back and re-wrote them. There were three articles in all and I shall never forget my thrill of pride as I saw them appear—with my name attached. This I gather was not always allowed, it was an honour; and as was explained to me afterwards, the publicity was considered the recompense,

and in a sense it was. For I did not make my fortune. I remember
I got £10 10s an article.

But it reminded my friends with a jolt that I was politically
still alive and Lady Bertha Dawkins, the Queen's Lady-in-Waiting, told me that at luncheon the first day my articles began to
appear, Queen Mary told King George that they were most in-
formative and well worth reading.

The King read them each day. People were so depressed about
our own unemployed and our own problems that they had not
realised how much worse and how much less well organised was
unemployment in the U.S.A. and I was asked on all sides to come
and tell study groups about the position. One such study group
was at Toynbee Hall, called the Enquirers Club. They not only
asked me there for dinner but we discussed the possibility of hitch-
hiking to study unemployment in England, Wales and Scotland.
I agreed and started out in December 1932. *The Times* had
agreed to publish what I saw, and did this in a further series of
Turnovers when I returned at the end of January 1933.

I have described this in a further book called *The Near-By
Thing*. I would like to quote what *The Times* said in a leader on
the subject on 4 February 1933. It was headed "The New Knight
Errantry" :

"Today Mr. William Teeling concluded the story of his
experiences as amateur tramp in England, Wales and Scotland. Last August he told of his corresponding travels in the
United States of America; and his British readers will be
entitled, for what it is worth, to this much of consolation—that
he found things much worse in that country than in this, and
greater general and particular effort to better them here than
there. His articles cannot fail to receive in high quarters the
practical consideration which they deserve. Meanwhile his
enterprise of itself throws light on modern conditions of life.
A journey in search of knowledge is no new thing in the country of Arthur Young and of others who were mentioned recently
in connection with the English travels of M. Francois de la
Rochefoucauld. About the lives of "trampers" as David
Copperfield called them when he tramped from London to

Canterbury, much has been learned from writers who—like Mr. W. H. Davies the "super-tramp" and Mr. George Orwell— have known tramping at first hand. But we come nearer to Mr. Teeling's kind of vagrancy with King Louis XI of France and the Caliph Haroun-al-Raschid of Bagdad, who disguised themselves and went amongst their people, not, indeed, with unmixed motives of the purest benevolence, but with a decent measure of goodwill.

"It is only in modern days, perhaps, that with the American, Josiah Flynt (Willard), with Mrs. Cecil Chesterton, with Mr. Frank Gray and Mr. William Teeling we reach this new and nothing ignoble form of errantry. While the world in general comes quite as close as it likes to rogues and vagabonds in the pages of Awdeley or Greene, of Jusserand or "The Cloister and the Hearth" these others become themselves rogues and vaga- bonds that they may learn how to help those whom fate. not choice, has made so. Of old the Knight-errant rode abroad, succouring virtue in distress, and with his own spear and sword beating down evil. Noble and arduous though it was, his task was simple compared with that of these new Knights-errant who cannot redress wrong singlehanded, but endure it and study it and make it known in a state of society where nothing less than the knowledge, the conscience, the power of a whole nation can contend with the evils that beset the whole nation."

In my book I explain that the statement I heard most often was one of the then Prince of Wales, in which he pointed out that if we look at unemployment as a whole we will be staggered by its vastness, and stand aghast at the immensity of our task—but if we all split it up into little bits with which we ourselves come into contact, then by all tackling our own little corner we will be able to fight this growing cancer successfully—in other words : "Do the near-by thing." Hence the name of my book.

The publication of this second round of articles and later my book, brought Questions in the Commons and the Minister of Labour, Rob Hudson, sent for me several times. Oddly enough, no Committee in the Commons asked me to tell them what I had seen. I was getting the impression that we had too big a majority and our Whips were not encouraging our M.P.s to be active on anything. The Archbishop of Canterbury, Dr. Lang, sent for me—but I was amused to find that he had not been too well briefed about me and thought that I actually was a "down and out" who somehow had caught the ear of *The Times*.

Next came the most interesting result; Geoffrey Lloyd, then one of Stanley Baldwin's P.P.S.s, told me that the Government were worried at the reports coming from abroad about the morale of our people and that they wanted someone to go through Europe to tell at least our own communities the real facts about the unemployed and the wonderful spirit they showed, plus the voluntary and other efforts which I had found were being made to help them.

I at once agreed. The next thing was how to organise it. Sir Evelyn Wrench, the head of the Overseas League and the founder of the English Speaking Union was approached by Mr. Rex Leeper of the Foreign Office. Both were imaginative men and Sir Evelyn said that he would put all the Branches of the League in France and Italy at my disposal to give lectures where I could. The Consular Service also decided to help and Mr. Deakin of *The Times* asked me to do two more articles, one on Unemployment in France and one on Unemployment in Italy. Our Ambassador, Lord Tyrrell, took the chair at my first meeting in Paris and I gave in both countries no less then twenty-five talks. We soon realised what a need there was for everyone, including our own residents abroad, to know more about facts at home. We seemed to have no propaganda abroad, though other nations were always at it. But once again where could the money be found? Leeper and Evelyn Wrench found the necessary money. Leeper was able to lay the foundation of what soon was to become the British Council and today one of the most flourishing organisations to show the flag for Britain.

CHAPTER IV

THE DAYS OF HITLER

W HEN THE National Government came to power in 1931, it is true that Ramsay Macdonald was in charge and there were in it such leading Labour lights—by now called National Labour—as Snowden and J. H. Thomas—but it was Stanley Baldwin's Government. It was always possible that he could decide to have a completely Conservative Government and even go to the country to get one. But those who knew what they were talking about told me that King George V, who had had a great hand in bringing about the coalition, was very averse ever to granting a Dissolution prior to one clear year after an election; and it must be remembered that this Government had the biggest majority since the Reform Bill of 1832 and seemed likely to run its full, or nearly full, course, say up to the spring of 1936 or the autumn of 1935.

I was not being very successful about getting adopted for a good seat; there were few going. The next election was too far off for the older Members to announce that they would not stand again. As there was such a big majority, and therefore so little to fight out in late night sittings in the Commons and such a feeble Opposition under the leadership of the little-known Attlee—chosen as Labour Leader only because there was no one else left except Lansbury—it seemed that very few Members with safe seats were dying. What should I do? I decided to continue my travels and explorations and a God-given opportunity came my way.

When I had gone to Canada I had joined the Overseas League for £1 1s., as its Secretary, a great friend Eric Rice, said to me: "It might be of use to you." When I got back in 1932 its Founder,

Sir Evelyn Wrench, as I have pointed out, offered the League to start up an experiment which eventually developed into the British Council. He had asked me to help by lecturing. The reports were evidently good and I had also helped him to get more Members for the League on the Continent; as the result I was made a member of their Council, the governing body. Their travelling Secretary became one of my greatest friends, Bob Lisle-Carr, son of the famous Bishop of Exeter who was criticised for holding some shares in Vickers, the armament manufacturers. As Randolph Churchill wittily remarked: "Tell the Bishop to hold on to his Vicars and I'm sure the Canons will take care of themselves." Bob used to tell me about his travels all over the world and the red carpet he had put down for him everywhere.

In 1934 Melbourne was about to celebrate its Centenary, and the Duke of Gloucester was to make it the occasion for a tremendous Australian tour. Cardinal MacRory was to go from Armagh to balance out the not very pro-British Archbishop Manning in Melbourne. The Army was to be represented by Field Marshal Lord Milne. The Overseas League's great rival the Royal Empire Society was to send its Chairman, Sir Archibald Weigall, ex-Governor of South Australia, and his wife; and who would the Overseas League send? The choice fell on a member of our Council, Lord Lloyd. Evelyn Wrench hated that sort of social gathering and would not dream of going himself. Then Lord Lloyd fell ill and in desperation the Council decided to ask me to go. But how could I afford it? The Council offered to pay all my expenses if in turn I would make it a sort of Lisle-Carr tour and make new members. I thought this over for some time. Here was a golden opportunity to see yet another part of the world and there seemed little likelihood of an election for over a year. I decided not only to take the risk but to make a further deal. I badly wanted to round off my experiences (as they would be after this) of migration possibilities to our White Dominions (South Africa only wanted richer migrants) by seeing our Colonies and how they compared with those of other great nations. It was a little known subject in this country. If the League would further pay my expenses to visit nearby parts of the world around Australia, I would guarantee to pay them back the balance owing, if I did not make enough members for the League during the tour to cover the expenses. The Council agreed and I set off.

Before I set out, Lady Annaly, an old and loyal friend of mine, wanted to arrange for me to meet the then Duke and Duchess of York. A party was duly arranged whereby the future King and Queen were to dine with the Annalys, we were then all to go to the theatre and later to dance at the Dorchester. I was put next to the Duchess of York at dinner. I remember so well one of her remarks at dinner: "You know I worry so much about what we can do for the Empire that sometimes I cannot sleep at night."

I had, a little before this, written a book in which I advocated that our Royal Family should do as did the Italian Royal Family, divide the country into spheres or areas and in each would go and live one member of the Royal Family and his wife and children. Evidently the Duke of York had read this and after dinner he said to me: "That is all very fine but on my State allowance how on earth could I afford to do this?" We do not realise how financially restricted are our Royalties. Just after the war, poor Princess Marie Louise was told by her doctors that she should go to somewhere on the Continent for a cure. But she told me it just was not possible on the official allowance and the King did not want her to set a bad example by applying for a greater allowance even though she would certainly have got it.

But to come back to that evening. We went on to the Dorchester and all went well until suddenly we saw the Prince of Wales arriving with Mrs. Simpson. After one dance the Yorks decided to leave and our party broke up.

Just before starting out for Australia I was summoned to the Yorks' house, 145, Piccadilly, for sherry and bitters with the Duchess before lunch. The Duke soon came in, his hand bandaged, it having been poisoned, and we had a long conversation about my coming visit.

Just before leaving, Princess Elizabeth came in with her Governess. It was the first time I met her. When I got to Australia, every day I was due to make a speech a telegram arrived in the morning with a message from the Duke of York. When we had spoken in London it had not seemed to me that he was particularly intent on my programme—but he must have got it

THE DAYS OF HITLER

later and that wonderfully efficient and charming person, Admiral Sir Basil Brooke, the Comptroller of his Household, must have got the dates and reminded him each time.

I was away for nineteen months, as usual I got tempted whilst away to make my tour more thorough and, by the time the 1935 Election did come along, I was buried in the depths of China, cut off by the Communists in the North, and once again without a seat worth coming back to fight! But I did visit all Australia, Queensland from Cairns and Townsville to Brisbane, Newcastle Downs and then down to New South Wales with Dubbo, Bathurst and the Broken Hill Mines thrown in, in addition to Sydney and Melbourne—not unnaturally since the tour centred around the Centenary; such parts of Victoria as Mildura where there were many of my Catholic Emigration settlers; Southern Australia and Western Australia right up *via* Geralton to the Kimberleys and on to Port Darwin.

It took me over six months—then I visited New Zealand and Tasmania and of Colonial Territories I went to Ceylon, Singapore, Malaysia, Papua, New Guinea, Fiji and Hong Kong. I compared notes by visiting French Indo-China (oddly enough as the guest of the then Colonial Secretary, the ill-famed Pierre Laval), Portuguese Macão, Dutch Sumatra and Java and Japanese Formosa. "Our India" as they proudly called it.

I added to this the Philippines, still under the U.S.A., a great deal of China and came home via the Trans-Siberian Railway. Once again I have written another book about this tour and I propose soon to go back to Australasia to compare notes with what I saw in 1934 and what it is like today, nearly forty years after.

Formosa, then Japanese and now Nationalist Chinese, deserves a book later on since I also went there as an M.P., as I have to explain later on, against the wishes of Anthony Eden and the Foreign Office.

I came back to find a much reduced majority in Parliament but one still pretty substantial, well over 200, and quite a few ex-M.P.s who had lost their seats and were likely to be my rivals in securing candidatures from then on. But I also arrived as the Nazis moved into the Rhineland, and as Oliver Stanley said to me not long after : "I realise that that was the moment when we should have put our foot down, but as the French would not budge and our own people just were not interested, there was nothing we could do." That Hitler was not ready, was bluffing and had not got the strength and would have withdrawn—we did not know then. I wonder why—where were our Intelligence people or were they just not listened to? The latter could be the case. The amount of good information that gets back to our Foreign Office and is just pigeon-holed always terrifies me.

On my return from the Far East in 1936 I moved into a lovely old house, No. 1, Swan Walk, Chelsea, eighteenth century and the original official residence of the Curator of the adjoining Physic Gardens. There I did a certain amount of entertaining, especially to Commonwealth visitors over for the Coronation who had entertained me on my travels. I was much helped by my M.P. friends.

I was made an offer by both the Rockefeller Foundation and the Royal Institute of International Affairs (Chatham House) namely, on a salary and with travelling expenses paid, to make a study of Nazi Germany (and Austria) and Fascist Italy to see whether it was possible to carry on the Catholic Church under each régime—a study to last two years.

I could now come back to look for and nurse a good seat. Indeed it became essential that I should come back pretty often, since it was not safe either for myself or for those I interviewed in Germany to take down notes—one's room was often searched and no one ever knew where were the hidden tape-recorders. The Bishop of Berlin, Cardinal Count Preysing, as he later became, always invited me into an inner room which he said he knew was safe and had no windows. One day when I was lunching in Eaton Place with the Oliver Hoares he told me that he was going to Berlin the following week to do an arms deal, I think for the Irish, and would be staying at the Bristol Hotel. I warned him : "Be careful, the bedrooms are wired." Princess Hohenlohe, then well-known as a supporter of the Nazis who was also at the luncheon blurted out, "That is not true, there is only one room wired there." Later she was to arrange for me to meet both Hitler and Hess at the Nuremberg Partei Tag and I had a most interesting time.

Only three things would I like to mention here, since I have also written a book on the religious and political sides of this problem. First when Edward VIII abdicated I came down from Hamburg to Berlin and with a friend listened to the Abdication broadcast. This friend was, I knew, a British spy in Berlin. He lived there and never wanted to leave, but he was suffering from cancer and he was terrified that whilst very ill or under drugs he might give away codes or secrets or tell of his contacts. Luckily he died before the war, but I have often wondered what people do under these circumstances?

The second thing was that the day following the Abdication, I was sent for by Hitler's great friend, Captain Wiederman, in the room next to Hitler's. He told me quite frankly that the German authorities were fully aware of all King Edward VIII's friends and had tried to cultivate them, but it had not dawned on them that he might abdicate. They knew nothing of the friends of King George VI and his Queen, could I help them by telling him? I saw no reason why not—if it meant for these only to be "cultivated" and I noticed (my third point) some of them were amongst those who were my fellow-guests at the Nuremberg Rally in 1937.

There is one thing which to this day worries me about Germany. Hitler said: "Give me ten years and I will have all the youth converted to my ideas." If we include the war years when presumably his education would have been more intense, he had his ten years. Are we to believe that everyone in Germany—or almost everyone—has dropped his theories? There were the Fuhrer Schools which I visited; there were the Ordenburgs which I visited. What has become of them all? German friends tell me that the old Hitler teachings are still certainly being taught.

Millions of presumably well trained Nazis, led by S.S. men, have left the East of Germany, hating as ever the Russians. They are now scattered throughout the West, but they have their political representatives working. I believe that there will soon be a new and alarming German Movement—a revival that we are not watching sufficiently. It may even be something that will be of use to a Europe slowly, at any rate in the East, being downtrodden by Communism. We should watch it all, because Parliaments do not seem to be any longer the answer, at any rate in some countries, to secure the freedom and culture and civilisation we all want. Just after the War, as an M.P. I went to battered Berlin. Some of those I met there said to me: "But why did you not join us in 1945 and sweep across Russia—it was the moment." These people must still be there and be more disillusioned than ever.

Whilst writing this book I have talked it over with many people, one of them Sir Oswald Mosley, now completely out of politics. I was struck by one of his comments which we might well remember. "Watch the Prussians; they are far and away the toughest of the Germans. They will certainly come back."

I also settled down to writing some books and produced one on *The Pope in Politics* and one on my Far East tour which was chosen by that brilliant Conservative, then running Ashridge College for the Tories, Sir Arthur Bryant, for publication as his "Book of the Month" in the National Book Club. *The Pope in Politics* was much criticised then as far too advanced and Left— today it would be considered ultra-Right. Victor Gollancz told me he was considering publishing for the Left Book Club the book *Gods of Tomorrow* which Arthur Bryant had chosen for his Right Book Club until Gollancz heard of this. It would have been unique as Left and Right!

Shortly after the Coronation I left my half of 1, Swan Walk which Robert Byron took over and kept until his tragic drowning during the war. Keith Winter, the playwright, lived in the other half of the house. He and Harold Acton, Brian Howard and Roger Spence, all still boys at Eton, edited their first review "The Eton Candle". I was already at Oxford and they made me get them their advertisements there. I moved to Albany, probably the most famous set of rooms, or Chambers as they are called, in the world. Gladstone, Bulmer Lytton, Byron, Clifford Bax, G. B. Stern and Macauley have all lived and written there. Between 1939 and 1940 whilst looking for a parliamentary seat, I produced there a book on Catholicism in Nazi Germany and one or two other semi-travel books all with the aid of one of the best

friends I have ever had, Michael Redmond, the perfect Secretary who today holds a key position in the Union side of the
Post and Telegraph Office. I loved my flat, K6, but it was half-
way along the Rope Walk and ladies coming to dinner complained
after leaving their cars at the Piccadilly entrance of the walk
along the Rope Walk, unsheltered on a windy night. Came the
War, and until I joined the Air Force I remained there with
occasional visits to our cellars for air raids. There never was much
of a view from my rooms, whereas where I have been until giving
up Parliament and where I put together the first notes for this
book, 88, St. James's Street, I was happiest. It was, oddly enough,
very quiet except for the changing of the sentries at St. James's
Palace and it has an unusually lovely view over St. James's
Palace. Every now and then one is woken by the fine Palace
Clock which, when it is working, starts striking at 6 a.m.

I always enjoyed a description of Albany in Marmion Savage's
novel *The Bachelor of the Albany* :

> "You know the Albany—the haunt of bachelors, or of mar-
> ried men who try to lead bachelors' lives—the dread of suspic-
> ious wives, the retreat of superannuated fops, the hospital for
> incurable oddities, a cluster of solitudes for social hermits, the
> home of homeless gentlemen, the diner-out and the diner-in,
> the place for the fashionable thrifty, the luxurious lonely, and
> the modish morose, the votaries of melancholy and lovers of
> mutton-chops."

It has not changed so very much and there are still politicians
living there, notably Edward Heath. It was from Albany that I
was summoned to be adopted for Bury in 1938.

After the Nuremberg Nazi Rally in 1937, at which I and
several Peers and M.P.s were present, and where I met both
Hitler and Hess and which greatly impressed me and also, quite
frankly, frightened me, I began to go less and less to Germany.
By 1938 at the time of Munich, I was already in Morocco, preparing for a journey down the West Coast of Africa—but it never
took place. General Noguès at the request of Georges Mandel
one of France's most brilliant Ministers, was looking after me.

Came the Munich crisis and he himself got a bit worried about the attitude of the various Moroccan chiefs in the mountains beyond Fez. He decided to visit them and he took me with him. It was an unforgettable experience. Noguès in early days had been Chef-de-Cabinet or A.D.C. to the great Marshal Lyautey. The Moroccans never forgot that and he had a warm welcome when, years later, he came back to represent France. His presence amongst the Chiefs had a very settling effect. I took many photos and three years later when I joined the Air Force, I asked their photographic section if they would like to borrow them. I found that they had none of the area we had been visiting. I tried to get them back the other day but they had been conveniently lost. I hope that they were at one time useful.

After the Munich crisis was over I left the General and moved south and later up the coast past Agadir to Mogador where I was told that for a few francs I could be shown the house where our new War Minister, Hore-Belisha, was born! I knew that he was a Jew but nothing else about his early days. A few years later, when I became M.P. for Brighton, I ran into his step-father, a retired civil servant knight called Hore and *not* a Jew. This Hore had married Leslie's mother and so he tacked on the Hore to his original name of Belisha. Still a few years later, when he had lost his seat in Parliament and was not having great success in finding another, he approached me indirectly through my fellow Brighton M.P., Tony Marlowe, to see if I would resign, so that he could walk into a safe seat. But I was too young then.

I was hardly back in London when Vansittart sent for me to the Foreign Office. He wanted me to go straight away on a British pep talk tour of Bulgaria and Rumania with Lady Maureen Stanley for the British Council. I had done one in Yugoslavia in 1936 and another in Norway, Denmark and Sweden in 1937. But this tempting trip was not to be, since an old friend, Humbert Wolfe at the Ministry of Labour, told me that we were just about to initiate a series of voluntary recruitment areas all over Britain to raise a body of people for Civil Defence. The country was to be divided into areas and every kind of preparation was to be made against invasion, in which civilians could help.

I was to be in control of a vast area, Cumberland, Westmorland, Northumberland, Yorkshire, Durham and Lincolnshire. I was to be directly under the Ministry of Labour in London but with two headquarters in the Ministry of Labour Offices at Newcastle-on-Tyne and Leeds. It was a fascinating assignment and I accepted at once. It lasted for six months and I had to speak at rallies, large—2,000/3,000 people—and small, in Leeds, Bradford (where I spoke with Compton Mackenzie who refers to the occasion in his latest book of memoirs), Pontefract, Newcastle and very many other places. It gave me a great insight into life in the North and in the different Civil Service offices and into the different kinds of hospitality (all most friendly), one could expect in the different kinds of homes.

When I got way out into Cumberland in mid-winter I arrived, frozen and badly in need of a drink, at the home of Lady Cecilia Roberts, the mother of Wilfrid Roberts, later a Liberal fellow M.P., who went to China with me. But I looked in vain for anything stronger than tea. Lady Cecilia was the daughter of the famous teetotaller and temperance leader, the Countess of Carlisle, who when her husband inherited Castle Howard and Naworth Castle had the priceless cellars of wines there taken out and poured down the drains.

By spring 1939 we had our organisations ready, but it was too late to go to Bulgaria and I set forth to start a weekly News-letter on the lines of Stephen King-Hall. This I later extended to a smaller one for children in the schools. It went well at first and I did most of my writing in my flat in Albany—but then came the war. I needed more financial backing and I got it very generously with no strings attached, other than that I should become a life member of the Royal Society of St. George and something quite high up in the Primrose League, from Lord Queenborough with whom I spent many interesting week-ends in the early days of the war. When, after Dunkirk, I joined the R.A.F. the News-letter, called *The British News Letter*, carried on for a few months with many friends nobly contributing supplements. But the Air Ministry frowned on it and so I had to pack it up.

CHAPTER V

LOOKING FOR SEATS

I T IS difficult to tell at what time in one's life frustration over-
takes one. You do not always realise it at the time. Looking
back now it seems clear that the war brought my greatest frustration. All the time and trouble which I had given to study conditions for migration comparing the different colonial systems,
looking at labour conditions at home during a terrible period of
unemployment and seeing what solutions other countries were
making in camps and the like, and lastly, studying the possibilities
of my Church maintaining its influence under Naziism and under
Fascism, all these things became out of date with the declaration
of war and we have looked at them differently ever since. Certainly I seemed to have wasted ten years of the best part of my life
and I remembered what Mrs. Neville Chamberlain had said: "Get
into Parliament in your early thirties if you wish to build up your
position." But I was forty-one the day after I got into Parliament.
Nevertheless I remained there throughout every upheaval until
I handed over two days after I was sixty-six, oddly enough to a
successor, Julian Amery, who was forty-nine on the day he was
elected.

When I returned from the Far East in March 1936 I was without a seat; had I had one at once, perhaps I could have put my
knowledge to better use—it was frustrating to start looking for
one all over again, but it may interest and encourage ex-M.P.s still
looking for seats and new aspirants to hear of my experience.

When I was first adopted in 1926 it was quite easy. The theory
then was that you fought a fairly hopeless seat; probably some
wealthy Tory either directly or indirectly paid for you to get your
experience. I wonder if under the new arrangements whereby

M.P.s are to tell who they may be working for outside Parliament it will mean that some of our more prominent, almost regular, Front Bench speakers, will have to declare who pays for them? It is still a good idea to fight hopeless seats whilst well under thirty. But you may get caught out. One Member I knew personally had a fairly flourishing business in the North and he was quite young. He was persuaded to stand in 1951 and was assured on all sides that he would never get in. But he did; and could not afford to give the time to come down to London during the week. The Whips insisted and the constituents had no intention of letting him resign. It did his business harm, but he was helped out. The Tories are more tolerant in this than Labour. I have seen a young ex-Labour M.P. come begging to the bar downstairs as a guest. He was down and out, but no one wanted to help except to give him a drink.

In recent years I went to British Guyana with a very charming Labour M.P. who got in first in 1964. His name was Alexander Garrow. He was Scottish and had a one man business; he had to neglect it; he had a heart attack and died in 1967 and his widow was left with little. There is a Parliamentary fund but it is very sparing in what it pays out to young or even old widows. You have to be ten years in the House before you are entitled to even a small pension.

Be that as it may, I set out on my renewed search in 1932, until I went East in 1934 and again when I got back in 1936. My first visit to Conservative Headquarters to make sure that I was still on the "Approved" Candidates' List, was not too encouraging. I must here explain that almost from the first day I was adopted, I was always dogged by another candidate, a most charming person, called Keeling. He was always just one ahead of me and the confusion between Keeling and Teeling was everywhere. Even when he married a most lovely redhead, one paper gave a full description of what life would be like for her, helping her husband in West Ham and North Woolwich, as a candidate. That was where I was standing—her husband was then in Woolwich on the other side of the river. Later he got Twickenham—very safe—joined the R.A.F. and rose to be a Squadron Leader—was knighted, and alas, finally died. He did all these things about

E

ten years ahead of me. But his widow, until she remarried, came often to my constituency, Brighton, as she adores Regency furniture and often turned up at London parties, as a widow, whilst I appeared alone as a widower. Many foreign ambassadors and even public announcers called us Sir William and Lady Teeling—or Sir Edward and Lady Keeling.

I paid my official call at Conservative Central Offices in 1936 to be greeted by Lord Windlesham whose job it then was, *inter alia*, to vet candidates. He was very charming and very deaf.

"My dear fellow, how nice to see you again. What can I do for you?"

This sounded encouraging. I knew that we had never met before; but still: "I've come, Lord Windlesham, to discuss getting a seat; if possible a fairly safe seat."

He looked at me as if I had gone off my head. "But my dear fellow why? You have already one of the safest seats in England. Has anything gone wrong?"

"No," I replied. "I have no seat at all at the moment."

Blank astonishment on the old boy's face. "But you are Keeling aren't you?"

"No, I'm afraid my name is Teeling."

"What? Stealing did you say? I'm afraid I'm a little deaf."

I tried to explain. He now seemed a little peeved.

"Oh! I'm sorry," he concluded. "I'm afraid that they've given me the wrong file. You must come again."

I did call a few weeks later and he was then ready for me. Born of a brandy family, Hennessy, he was a Catholic and he made the interesting comment: "You know we Catholics, also Jews, always find it most difficult to get safe seats. You see the selection committees usually boil the candidates down to a last three or four and there are very few Catholics who are more outstanding than some intelligent and eligible members of the Church of England. It is usually the ladies on the Committee who will then say: 'Well Mr. X is really about as good as Mr. Y and a lot of people in our Party don't like R.C.s or Jews, so let's play safe and have Mr. X'."

He was, in those days, right and as I went up and down the country I found this to be very much the case. Sometimes I was not even interviewed, as at Newbury, where the Chairman was Sir Arthur Griffith-Boscawen. I thought that I had a pull there since his sister, Mrs. Taaffe, was married to my cousin and had become an R.C. to marry him—but no, it had made him even more anti-R.C. and he told her he would never let my name go forward.

In a Birmingham seat I got into the last two where my predecessor had been an R.C. but some of the Committee said: "We don't want another one." Now I see that seat has gone Labour and has a Jewish Member.

Up and down the country I went, a real carpet bagger, just as they are today. There were about nine of us who always seemed to be chosen by the Committees to be interviewed. One's heart sank as one got on the train and saw the familiar faces at the carriage windows; but we all knew each other well and were friends and began to think that we knew where the others had gone wrong at the last selection meeting. We were rather like the ten little nigger boys; as each new visit took place we were always one less.

I remember in the front, Ian (now Lord) Fraser, Reggie Manningham-Buller (now Lord Dilhorne), Derek Walker-Smith, John Maude and so on. Central Office usually asked you if you would like your name sent forward; or you wrote to Central Office and asked for your name to be included. From then on you had to pull your own strings. I remember one constituency where Dennis Vosper later became the Member. The Central Office list had not arrived by the evening the Selection Committee was to meet. Vosper was the Agent and the Committee knew he wanted to stand, so they let him be chosen straight away.

I would give this as a tip to many. There always used to be Agents' Courses at Ashridge and there still are at Swinton. I used to manage to get asked to go and talk to them on my experiences. These Agents were always on the look out for suitable candidates should anything happen to those they already served; and also, being human, they would like to see some of these candidates who were only names to many of them and to sum up just how easy it would be to work with them, or dare I say it, even to run and boss them. I always therefore tried to look as if

I would be an easy type to control. Some fell for this, and through those meetings I often found myself short listed, but there was always the religious hurdle to get over.

Finally came the day when it looked as if I would get Bury in Lancashire. The Agent, Moorhouse, had helped quite a bit. The seat, however, was in the midst of the area which could well be called Lord Derby's influence; without his backing it would, I was assured, be hopeless. I had one near rival, and this is where the luck of the draw comes in. It was Ralph Etherton who was, I think, the nephew of the Chief Constable of Lancashire.

I did not know Lord Derby but I knew both his sons, his son-in-law and particularly his daughter-in-law, Lady Maureen Stanley, Robin Castlereagh's sister. I went to her, she wrote to Lord Derby who was at that moment on the Riviera and his son-in-law Malcolm Bullock was stopping with him. Between them I got his backing. Came the final day and I'm told once again the stumbling block was my religion—but the leading Trade Unionist on our Selection Committee said : "What's it matter, if he's good enough for Lord Derby he's good enough for us," and in the final count I was adopted unanimously. It was only a few weeks after that I heard on the wireless that my old Magdalen friend, Anthony Crossley, M.P. for Stretford, also in Lancashire, had been killed in an air crash. Stretford was possibly the most Catholic constituency then in Lancashire. A few weeks earlier and I would probably have got it and been in Parliament in six weeks. Instead of which there I was, adopted for Bury and might have to wait nearly another year. Stretford said, "Well Etherton was runner up for Bury, let's have him," and in he went as M.P. for Stretford.

"Bury is different," was a saying I often heard whilst I was "nursing it". It was the only seat in the neighbourhood which had remained Tory in 1929 and again in 1945 and right up to 1964. It seemed rather an oasis of semi-feudalism around which had grown the lack of character of Manchester buildings. The President of the Conservative Association, Myles Kenyon, was also the head of the firm employing probably most people in the area. He came second only to Lord Derby in local influence, was also a very well-known cricketer, and lived well away from the constituency in an attractive house in Gloucestershire. Next probably in importance was Canon Hornby, the local vicar, whose living was, I believe, in the gift of Lord Derby who was his kinsman. Canon Hornby had a son whom I did not meet, but who later became M.P. at a by-election for Tonbridge. Today, the younger Hornby is an outstanding member of the Left in the Conservative Party. I sometimes find it frightening to sit next to him at any Right Wing dinner. He resents so much what is said and mutters about it so loudly that I often fear an explosion. No doubt he will go far if the Tories are returned under their present leadership.

Next in importance in the then Tory hierarchy, was the Chairman of the Association, Dr. Rothwell, than whom there was no nicer or kinder man—but he had no great sympathy with the sitting Member, Alan Chorlton. In fact, once I came on the scene he, Kenyon and Lord Derby did what they could to get Chorlton to retire as he had promised to do at the "coming Election", i.e. in 1939, the Election that never was. But probably my greatest help and the man most sympathetic to my mind was Tom Walmsley. I think that everyone liked him. His business was really just as important as Kenyon's and he and his wife had a delightful house on the edge of the constituency where it was a great relief to get away at week-ends. His son-in-law, Alan Green, followed me into the House and as one of the M.P.s for Preston rose quite high in a short time. He seemed and seems, since I understand he is standing again, to have quite a future and a delicious dry sense of humour.

The Catholic Parish Priest was, of course, of importance to to me since at the previous General Election, Edith Summerskill had stood against Chorlton and gone all out for birth control. There was a Catholic vote of some 5,000 votes then in Bury and they all plumped for Chorlton. Edith took it very badly at the Count. I did about a year of canvassing, mostly Clubs. I cannot say that I was really happy there; unlike Brighton it was the sort of constituency that made you want to do your real work at Westminster and only get back to canvass. But I understood my successor was a far greater success and he certainly was a brilliant asset to the House.

I refer to Walter Fletcher. He was not a good-looking man but he was absolutely brilliant, spoke French like a native, was an international businessman and knew China backwards. I was always enthralled by his conversations in the House. He coined for me the phrase *"Marché-parallele"* which he said was more appropriate for the French than in talking of them as being adepts at the use of the *"Marché noir"*. On China he was convinced that the whole area was far too big to be one nation and that it must break up one day into North and South—with Chiang Kai-shek probably in charge of the South at Canton. Alas he is dead. He was succeeded by Bidgood who did not make quite such an impact on the House. He went about all the time with two other M.P.s one of them, Farey-Jones, a man who had unexpectedly won an unlikely seat without any real help from Central Office and who seems to be extremely well-known in many parts of the outside world, especially Spain. He started our first Anglo-Spanish Group, but he never seemed to get any recognition from the Party.

All three of them I managed to get out to Formosa as the guests of the Taiwan Government. They just would not go alone; they became known as our Three Musketeers. Farey-Jones when he came back had long talks with Alec Home at the Foreign Office about recognising Chiang Kai-shek but without success. Bidgood eventually lost Bury and the present Labour M.P. a former Mayor, was quite popular until he got us all involved in that hot potato "ritual slaughter" which always brings out Jewish and R.S.P.C.A. feelings. But I understand he is not standing again.

About this time I was walking along Piccadilly when I ran into Harold Macmillan. I told him cheerfully that I would soon be with him in the House as Member for Bury.

"You won't you know," he replied gloomily. "There's going to be a war very soon and there'll be no Election."

How right he was! There was no Election and the sitting Member, Alan Chorlton, who had told us all how unwell he was, now suddenly felt better and never resigned until the General Election of 1945. Lord Derby tried hard to press him to go but he would not and I looked as if I would be left all through another war, just an adopted candidate. But the Bury Conservatives sportingly said : "Look elsewhere if you like, but we will keep the seat for you." At least they said this up to 1943. I had joined the R.A.F. and was away and by then they had got tired of me.

I started to look around once again and the Agent for Brighton suggested I put my name forward there as one of their joint Members, Lord Tryon, had just been made a Peer. This was in 1940. But the price to pay for Brighton was a little steep. You would be expected to pay off all the Association's debt (about £1,000); you were, of course, (everybody did then officially) to pay your election expenses and you were to pay to the Association £600 a year. Lastly, you were to take a house in the constituency which must be big enough to be able to give two garden parties (paid for by me !) a year.

I agreed on the Brighton terms but I only got sixth on the list. The Chairman was one of the Colman mustard family and I had not much impressed him. Lord Erskine, a former Whip and just back from having been Governor in Madras, got it. Neville Chamberlain had been backing him and had promised him office if he got in. Poor Erskine, whose wife's family, the Bristols, owned a large part of Brighton in the Kemp Town end, had to pay off the debts, but avoided the Election expenses since there was a Party truce for the war. As everyone was being asked to evacuate Brighton and seaside towns if they could, he argued that to take a house would be setting a bad example. His wife told me afterwards that the Association was so snobbishly run there that you could never meet the average person or get out to any meeting.

He was soon at loggerheads with the Executive and by 1941 he threw his hand in. Things were rather different now. Most eligible candidates were scattered overseas. I was stationed in Ulster and asked to come back and see the Association again. I did this but I had one close rival. He was a friend of the Colmans and I was a friend of the Vice-Chairman and the Treasurer, Colonel Peters, a brewing magnate, and Mr. Andrews, a publican. When it came to the final decision I was told that why Brighton would not have me was because I was not married. I pointed out that I was actually engaged and that I would be married by the following January, 1942. It was no use—I was runner up but not in. Anthony Marlowe got it with his fascinating wife, a daughter of Patrick Hastings the Socialist K.C.

Before leaving, however, I was told that the other Member for the constituency—in those days there were such things as two Member seats—was not likely to remain on very long. He would soon be twenty-one years the local M.P. and might well retire. Actually, during the next year he had a stroke and quickly withdrew. This would be the third Election poor Brighton (which of course also included Hove) would have since the war started. The debts had been paid off, there was no further effort at M.P.s entertaining and as there was a Party truce, there would not be any election expenses. This constituency had had a 62,263 majority in 1931—the biggest in the history of England and it was only down to 41,626 in 1935. It really was tempting. Colonel Peters was now the Chairman and he told Sir Thomas Dugdale (now Lord Crathorne), the Party Chairman, that only a year ago I had been runner up and had been turned down for not being married. Since then I had got married and to a wife whose grandfather had been a Whip and Lord of the Treasury in Gladstone's day, so surely there was no need to go before another Selection Committee?

I was by then working at the Air Ministry. I went to see Lord Baldwin. He agreed that maybe I was getting a bit old for the regular type of pre-war "running in" as an M.P., but that once I was in we could see whether I could not get a good Colonial governorship which was what I felt I might now be most suitable for and where I might help in post-war changes. Little did we know the 1945 policy! Anyway, the wheels were set in motion. My chief at the Air Ministry, Lord Stansgate, gave me the necessary permission commenting: "I expect you will get in, after all we have not held Brighton since 1910." I reminded him that in 1910 he was a Liberal and now he was a Socialist Peer and no Socialist had ever held Brighton—I spoke just twenty-one years too soon!

I was adopted—and then ten days later all Hell broke loose.

Within twenty-four hours the criticisms were starting. I was a Roman Catholic; it was the very centre of English Protestantism.

I was Irish; and although I was in our own Air Force I came from Southern Ireland which was neutral. I was locally unknown and this would be the third local by-election since the war started. Each candidate chosen had been an outsider and no local representative even interviewed. My fellow-Member, Colonel Marlowe, was in the Army it was true; but only on the legal side, the Judge Advocate's department. I was in the R.A.F. but I did not have wings. I was what an indignant retired Air Marshal called "chairborne" at the Air Ministry. Still, it was agreed between all three Parties that during the war there would be no contested elections. It would be unheard of in such a loyal centre as Brighton that the agreement would be disregarded and so we waited for the morning when I would hand in my papers (by twelve mid-day), and, nobody opposing, I would be duly declared elected. My wife and I went, pretty confident, to the Town Hall. I had been to a boxing match the night before with the Mayor and had thought he looked a little uncomfortable.

Suddenly, seven minutes before the deadline, to our horror, into the Mayor's Parlour walked his own brother, Bernard Dutton-Bryant, and handed in his papers and deposit. He had as his chief backer the Mayor of the other part of the constituency, the Mayor of Hove. My Agent went white in the face. We had heard nothing of this. Mayors never took an active part in politics; it could only mean that there was the strongest feeling. Soon it was known all over England and of course in enemy Germany. Churchill was being flaunted; I was being opposed by an Independent, a local barrister, a member of the Sussex Yeomanry, a brother of the Mayor and member of a leading Liberal family. Officially, he said, he was also a supporter of Churchill, but was only objecting to the third carpet bagger in three years trying to become Brighton's M.P.

There was no constituency money problem like there would be today for a by-election. In those days the candidate had to find the money himself—but the Register of Electors was hopelessly out of date; there was no absent voters list. We were in the middle of a war, everything blacked out after dark—and it was January. No one could walk along the front, no one was allowed to come into Brighton by car or by train without a permit. Nearly half the population—my voters and presumably supporters—had been evacuated. It certainly was a pretty kettle of fish. Talk of frustration! That evening I held my first public meeting. I was in the uniform of a Flying Officer and of course had to get into civilian clothes. Lady Apsley, M.P. was rushed down from London to speak for me and would keep on calling me Flight Officer—which is a woman's rank and as the town had many Air Force types, Australians and others training here—that was another joke to be laughed off. My wife and I moved into the only hotel functioning with rooms to spare, the Bedford, and there I found our Communist from Magdalen, Wogan Philipps—later to become the only Communist Peer as Lord Milford—on his honeymoon with his wife, Lady Huntingdon, who also had been at Oxford with me, as Christina Casati. Every evening they sat and laughed in the hall as they saw me and my friends (mostly theirs as well) go out to my meetings in the blackout.

It was an election I would not wish for my worst enemy. We had really been caught with our pants down. I was unknown; my opponent was well known. He had the support of all, or nearly all, the best known businessmen in the town led by a brilliant speaker, Alderman Aldrich; and Charles Wakeling, the head of the Football Club and of the dog racing. There was practically no one to canvass and anyway there never had been any canvassing done in the old days—everything had been so safe. Duncan Sandys, Malcolm McCorquodale, Liberals and Socialists, J. P. L. Thomas, considered Eden's right hand man—they all came down to speak for me night after night and almost every night there was an air raid warning whilst we were speaking and down we had to go to the dug-outs for the schools in which we were speaking. Everything was blacked out. Then came the uncertainty of which papers were supporting me and the *Brighton Herald* refused to publish Churchill's letter of support. I too was warned by the then Solicitor General, David Maxwell-Fyfe, not to publish it as in his opinion it was both libellous and defamatory: Dutton-Bryant would be too clever to sue Churchill but would almost certainly sue me. I therefore never published it, but here it is and it had already been given to the National Press before I got it!

10, Downing Street,
Whitehall

28th January 1944
Dear Mr. Teeling,

As the Conservative candidate unreservedly supporting the National Government, you have my cordial wishes for success in this by-election.

Your opponent who styles himself as Independent, is reported to claim that "he stands in full support, of the Prime Minister and the Cabinet". I am sure that the electors of Brighton and Hove will not be taken in by this attempted swindle.

Why has the nation weathered the fiercest storm in its history? It was only by standing together. Our unity must not be lost while we are still beset with perils and privations.

Evidently we stand on the threshold of world events. The electors of Brighton who have been in the front line of air attack and invasion threat from the Battle of Britain till now, should tell the country that this is no time for political antics.

I ask them to return you to Parliament by a majority which will help us forward on our road.

Yours sincerely,
WINSTON S. CHURCHILL

The bit about the "swindle" was the dangerous bit. Feeling locally mounted fast over the next few days, my wife championing me nobly found herself in many a heated scene—for she too was locally unknown.

A group of Protestant organisations, mainly non-conformist, banded themselves together and took considerable space in the local papers asking people not to vote for a Papist. I began to feel, incredible though it might seem with a majority in 1935 of over 41,000, that I might yet lose the seat. Attlee had written in support of me, so had the National Liberal Leader and cartoons were appearing in the National Press—one showed me incredulous as the postman had no letter of support to deliver to me. The caption was: "You can't expect one every day."

I decided one afternoon in the Union Club in Brighton, where we had a telephone call-box into which you put 1/6d. for London, to ring up James Stuart, the Chief Whip. After I had spoken to him for a couple of minutes, and had told him that I needed yet another letter from the P.M., he said : "You had better speak to him yourself; he is just here." Within seconds I was speaking to the well-known voice. He was kindly and helpful and promised to write to me once again.

Whilst this was going on a small female voice piped in and said : "Another 1/6 please or I must cut you off."

I replied : "You can't; I'm speaking to the Prime Minister."

"I don't care who you are speaking to. Another 1/6d please."

The P.M. went on for nearly fifteen minutes and wretched Club bridge players were rushing backwards and forwards collecting shillings and sixpences until the end.

Next day I got another letter in which Churchill said that it had been brought to his attention that he had never meant to say such things about my opponent, but he wished to make it clear that he had meant it and stood by every word he had said. Lord Donegall sent me a wire saying : "You silly ass, why did you not reverse the charges?" From then on Lord Beaverbrook more or less took charge of my publicity and rang me every morning in my office about 10 a.m. This other well-known voice always started off with "Are you alone in the room" and then went on to give me his information and his advice.

I was told later that he had had someone else in mind for the seat but the Chief Whip and the Party Chairman had persuaded Churchill to support me. If that was so, it was very big hearted of Beaverbrook to go all out to support me towards the end. He had felt that I was not perhaps so whole-heartedly behind Churchill as he would have liked and that this was partially because I never mentioned Churchill once in my Election Address. The Address was actually written for me by Mr. Hooper, who was backing the Tory Reform Group at that time; he was a former partner of Lord Woolton and later the head of Schweppes.

For my Eve of the Poll meeting in the Music Room at the Brighton Pavilion—then a rather shabby room—I had Florence Horsbrugh as my chief speaker and she certainly did one proud. On coming in, I was met at the door by Joe Hogan, head of

A.T.1 at Air Ministry who lived in the constituency. He brought the best wishes of all my Air Ministry friends; it cheered me a lot; I needed it. He told me, only the other day, how scared he was by what he heard all through the town.

Next day we polled. People were standing outside polling booths telling electors not to vote for me because I was a Catholic. All this religious and anti-Irish feeling had greatly worried the local Jews; there were many of them and they were very powerful. It sounded alarmingly like anti-Jewish feeling, and they all rushed around on the last two days doing all they could to help. I calculated there were about 6,000 of them then in the town.

The count was quite sick-making and at one moment a whole ballot box for an area which I calculated was safe was mislaid. This soon was righted and I was in—in by 2,309—a very great difference from 1935 and the 41,000 majority. Still I had made it.

Eighteen months later, at the General Election, and before the people evacuated had returned, I got in by 18,265, an increased majority of 16,000 at a time when everything elsewhere was going against our Party—this was not noticed in the national debacle, but it was by me—whereas the whole period from February 1944 until the dissolution in 1945 I felt that I was looked on as "the man who made Brighton marginal". Even Churchill, when I was about to march up the centre of the Commons to take my seat, rather pointedly walked out. He never sent me a word of congratulation and the *Evening Standard* commented on his "stalking out".

Later I was to hear a story from Bill (Lord) Astor which may or may not be true—but it seems to have some foundation in it. Churchill had recently been very ill in Morocco. Another bout of pneumonia, it was felt, and he might well succumb. Many in the Cabinet wanted Eden to succeed and wanted him to succeed without any election or difficulty. Here were three by-elections coming up in spite of the truce; mine, one in Suffolk, and one in Derbyshire. Churchill was demanding loyalty and confidence. If we lost all three or even two, Churchill might straight away be persuaded to go to the country and gain a fresh mandate. Then, were he to fall ill again, Eden could step into his shoes at what would be the beginning of a new Parliament. What Labour would do was not very clear. I certainly nearly lost the seat and many wondered at the intrigues against me. Poor Lord Hartington, married to President Kennedy's sister, definitely did lose what was considered a Cavendish stronghold and went back to the Front to be killed; and a Suffolk seat was not easily won either.

The next year in France, relations of mine living in Bordeaux, whose house had been taken over by the Germans so that they were left to use three rooms only, told me how they had that night been listening to the radio from Paris. They heard that Churchill's nominee had been very nearly defeated in a by-election and was called Flt. Lieut. Teeling and that this showed how his influence was waning. This was the first they had heard that I was still alive and that I was in the Air Force and in Parliament.

This is a Churchill story too. It was a week or so after I got in that Churchill's anger having blown away, he went up to my poor friend, Squadron Leader Keeling (who thought Churchill knew him well, at least by sight) in the Smoking Room, offered him a drink and said how sorry he was if that letter had done him harm in the by-election. He asked him to tell him all about it. Two different Ministers, who were sorry about my experiences, sent me invitations to little parties they were having. They did not happen to be friends of Keeling and he was amazed to receive their invitations instead of me—the Messengers had not "placed" me yet.

The next thing to happen to me was even more maddening. I had for about a year had a fascinating job at Air Ministry. I went every morning at 9.30 to the meeting of the Air Council. At this meeting was reported in full everything concerning the air activities of the last twenty-four hours; this was followed by a report from a representative of the Admiralty and from the War Office. After this I went with my notes to work out what would most interest our Air Attachés in neutral countries such as Sweden, China, Turkey and Spain—in fact, everywhere where we had one. These would then be vetted by Group Captain Lionel Heald, later M.P. for Chertsey, and sent by code so that our Air Attachés could dine out and keep their ears open to hear what others knew. I shared a room with my old Magdalen Oxford friend, John Strachey—by now a Socialist. Whilst I was out of the room he was always ringing up Dundee to see how his candidature was going on and, whilst he was out of the room, I would be ringing up Brighton—the State paid!

But the moment I became an M.P. I lost that all enlightening job. It was far too dangerous for an M.P. to know so much. I was posted to our section at the Ministry of Information.

CHAPTER VI

THE WAR AND IRELAND

ARLY IN 1940 I was turned down for the R.A.F. as being
not medically fit (at thirty-six) but at the same time I
had just been passed fully fit for an insurance policy; this
made me pretty mad. After all, I was not trying at that age to
become a pilot and so I went to my old friend, Keeling, by now
in the Commons and also in the R.A.F., and within weeks he
had cut the red tape and I was commissioned a Pilot Officer in
the R.A.F.V.R. and straight away turned into an Intelligence
Officer. This was just a few months before every recruit had to
go through a very tough training course to be an officer.

I had volunteered and been, I gathered, accepted, because of
my knowledge of the Far East and especially Japan. As a result,
within a few weeks I was posted over to Northern Ireland and,
had it not been for a piece of luck in 1942, I think that I would
have stopped there for the rest of the war! I was posted to Aldergrove on the edge of Lough Neagh from Fighter Command, to
look after the only Fighter Squadron there. We were what is
called a Lodger Unit on the then only R.A.F. Station in Northern
Ireland, a Coastal Command Station and the headquarters of
the Ulster Auxiliary Squadron 502. I had managed to sub-let
my flat in Albany and my father was safely in Dublin, aged
eighty-three. I presumed he would stay there—but he got bored
and came back to England to die in Tunbridge Wells in 1943,
just three months before I was elected M.P. for Brighton.

On arrival in Ulster—or, as it is officially called, Northern
Ireland—I went straight to my new Station, Aldergrove. I
scarcely knew Northern Ireland then. Our next door neighbour
in Dublin had been Sir John Ross of Bladensburg who was the

5. Luncheon Group at the Irish Embassy, London, on the occasion of the Agreement regarding the Lane Collection of Paintings.

Left to Right: Hector Hughes, Q.C., M.P., Lord Pakenham, Professor Thomas Bodkin, Hugh McCann (Irish Ambassador), Lord Moyne and the Author.

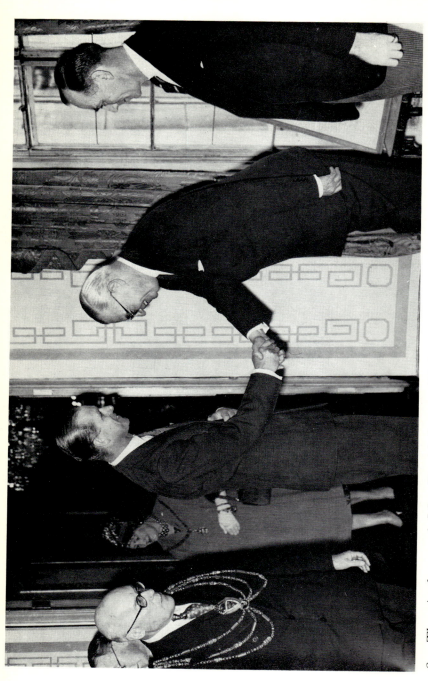

6. The Author and Mr. David James, M.P. for Kemp Town, welcome Prince Philip at the Brighton Pavilion, 1962.

head of the police—the Royal Irish Constabulary—during the
First World War, when I knew him and his delightful wife, a
sister of the then Lord Massereene and Ferrard. They were
Catholics (converts), a most unusual thing amongst the gentry
in Ulster, and my parents and I used to stay with them at their
lovely place at Rostrevor. The first time we went was on 12 July,
Orange Day, and at the station was an Orange Band—not meant
for us!

It is only now, since the terrible troubles in Ulster in 1969 and
Miss Bernadette Devlin's colourful entry into the Commons, that
most people realise what can happen in the North. I have always
known about this and so have my ancestors, but a description
of how I personally found it from 1940 to the end of 1942 will
give a background and help explain how this may affect the
United Kingdom and Parliament over the next few years.

I was hardly at Aldergrove before I was called on by the local
Parish Priest at Crumlin. He happened to be quite a scholar and
knew a lot about Irish history and also about my own family. He
motored me over to Lisburn where my great-great-grandfather
lived and was arrested. He showed me the place where until
about 1910 our house had stood, slightly on a hill now where the
convent stands, and he showed me many places connected with
my family. The most important family in that area was, and still
is, the Barbour family. Sir Milne Barbour was a member of the
Government. The priest also knew that the Barbours and the
Teelings had been the biggest local people in the flax and linen
industry of that area. There was no religious prejudice in the
Barbours' home and Sir Milne often had me to stay for week-
ends. When I married, he gave a big dinner party for my wife
and me.

I also went to stay with Lord Glentoran, yet another member
of the Government. I was playing bridge with him after dinner
on the Saturday night.

Lady Glentoran came over to me and said : "Would you like
to be taken to Mass in the morning?"

Lord Glentoran put his cards down and looked me straight
in the face : "You're not a Roman Catholic are you?"

He looked horrified.

F

"There's only one Roman Catholic who goes to Mass from this town and that's X [mentioning someone from the South whom I knew well] and he only goes because he badly needs it to save his soul."

He was half-joking and Lady Glentoran herself motored me to Church. But in the two years I was there I was never asked into that house again.

I often went for week-ends to Lord and Lady Londonderry at Mount Stewart and there they insisted that I should go to Mass—but the car deposited me at the bottom of a hill near where the church was built. I had to walk the last lap and on the way back I again walked down to the main road and was driven back to lunch. It seems that when the two Infantas, daughters of King Alfonso XIII stayed with the Londonderrys and the car drove them to the church door, there was nearly a riot in Newtownards, the local town.

Years later when the Londonderrys' Keppel grand-daughter married a Catholic at the Brompton Oratory in London, the local Mayor of Newtownards was nearly drummed out of the Orange Order for attending the Service, but got off by pleading that as the Londonderrys owned most of the town it was his duty as Mayor to attend; but Mrs. Nigel Fisher, who lived near and had been herself M.P. for that area of Ulster, who also attended, was expelled.

Let us, however, be fair on this. At the beginning of the century there was the most frightful fuss when Edward VII and Queen Alexandra went to a Requiem Mass for the assassinated King of Portugal in 1908; even later, the Pope's representative at George VI's Coronation had a special box built for himself just outside Westminster Abbey, and none of my family were ever allowed to attend a wedding in a Protestant church in Southern Ireland.

When I was married at Lucan, just outside Dublin, my best man was a Protestant, the Marquess of Donegall. I heard rumours the night before that the Parish Priest was objecting to a Protestant being on the Altar and so I told my wife's cousin, Roderick More O'Ferrall who is a Catholic and who was organising the ushers for me, to keep an eye out, as I would be on the Altar being married and would not be likely to see what was going on. If anything went wrong he promised to step in. Sure enough, just as Donegall was coming forward to hand me the ring, the Parish Priest who was not marrying us (my brother-in-law, a Jesuit, was doing this), stopped him coming forward and Roderick quickly took over. Next day the *Irish Times* reporting the wedding said that "The best man was the Marquess of Donegall", but the *Irish Independent* said that the best man was Mr. Roderick More O'Ferrall. Donegall, who in those days was writing a well-known column in the *Sunday Dispatch* called "Almost in Confidence", spread a headline the next Sunday called "I was stopped at the altar".

There is much more in the problems of Ulster than just Catholic versus Protestant—the history of the place will show that. A middle-aged priest not from the border counties but from the interior of Ulster, Antrim, told me that, when he went to the South for his holiday to Mayo or right down to Cork, of course he spoke the same language of his faith; but what is important is that he never felt happy either with the priests of the South or even with the laity. There was a difference; and it wasn't just religion. They were different people; he always felt a stranger and the longer you have been in the North the more you realise this truth—its in the Provinces' history, however few people there are; it is something like the Walloons and the Flemish in Belgium.

Expressed differently, but on the same theme, it was put to me by Lord Craigavon, then Prime Minister. He pointed out that Ulster had never been more peaceful or contented as since Partition. I must say, and I was in charge of security at Aldergrove, he was in those days of the war, correct. Ireland was in a strange position at that time. Southern Ireland was neutral and Ulster was well in the war. Yet there were far more recruits fom Southern Ireland for our Forces, mostly coming to Belfast to enlist, than there were from Northern Ireland. The Northern Irish were working in the factories, in Harland & Wolfe and were earning good money, and they let the British come over and train and prepare for battle, but we found it difficult to get recruits.

When I arrived at Aldergrove it was small and compact. It

was, as I have said, the only air field in Northern Ireland. This was just after Dunkirk and during the Battle of Britain. We were at first told that the country was too boggy, too sodden to lay down runways and everything would have to be done from Aldergrove. Soon we began to get reports of German planes over neutral Southern Ireland and then coming up the Channel and turning into the U.K. Our Coastal Command aircraft did their best, but somehow and regardless of cost we must get far more air fields. The first we started was for Fighters at Ballyhalbert, almost on the Strangford Lough. Then we started others at Eglinton near Londonderry and still more Coastal Stations for seaplanes at Castle Archdale on Lough Erne and at St. Angelo, the Bishop's Palace in that area. It was my not-very-pleasant job, having gone round the countryside with a delightfully sympathetic character, S/Ldr. Murgatroyd, to choose possible sites, to call on the wretched owners of the local big houses in these places and to tell them that we must requisition their homes and their land and as far as they themselves were concerned, turn them out.

When we took over Ely Lodge (today the home of the Duke of Westminster) and saw Lord and Lady Ely, none too pleased, eating in an hotel on the Lough, how was I to know that Lady Ely came from Brighton and Hove and that in a couple of years I was to find her and her husband there and I their Member of Parliament! The place I most hated taking over was Nutts Corner on the road from Belfast to Aldergrove, when there were just a few small cottages where the owners had lived for ages. It had to be done; they were pulled down and today this is the Civil Airport for Belfast.

At Aldergrove, one of my first security problems was to explain the strange lights which seemed to appear from across Lough Neagh at night, in spite of the blackout. Twice I was sent over in a speedboat (the noise of which would scare anyone away who was up to no good). I was authorised to take a revolver and told not to fire unless "they" did first. It wouldn't have done much harm if I had, since I had never used a revolver in my life. I, of course, found nothing. I then motored over to see Dame Dehra Parker, one of the most efficient women in Ulster and in the

Government. She lived on the other side of the lough and knew every inch of it.

In the end we discovered that all these lights and signals had nothing to do with war, but merely with poaching and with a long dispute concerning the fishing rights of Lough Neagh, going back a century. The poachers pointed out that, anyway, if we were talking about the non-observance of the blackout regulations, I had better look over at our own air field. How right they were; it seemed a blaze of light. It was while I was over there visiting Dame Dehra in 1941 that I first met her grandson, Robin Chichester-Clark. He was then aged thirteen and reminded me of it when he got into the Commons in 1955 where he has been an outstanding success in a very difficult position since he is now leader of the Ulster Unionist M.P.s. His elder brother is Ulster's new Prime Minister. These two brothers have more of their grandmother's political flair than many realise.

Not very long after I went to Aldergrove the Station Commander sent for me and said: "Be ready tomorrow morning any time to receive a number of aircraft and pilots flying in from the United States or Canada. No one will be in uniform. They will want some food and you are to take them to the Grand Central Hotel, Belfast, where rooms will be reserved for them. The utmost secrecy is to be observed as to where they have come from." No more; I don't think that he knew any more himself.

They arrived early; they looked the most incredible bunch of seeming-toughs, in every kind of garment—some in Wild West garments, others like the future leader of the Pathfinders, Air Marshal Bennett, in his Imperial Airways Captain's uniform and all one hundred per cent American or Canadian. It was an historic occasion. It was the first contingent of American Lend-Lease aircraft to be flown secretly to our aid from across the Atlantic and before the U.S. joined us.

We went into Belfast to the Grand Central. Promptly the receptionist refused to give them rooms until they filled in the usual forms stating where they came from and where had they spent the night before. This took me quite a bit of telephoning to straighten out. Then the A.O.C. Sir Robert Carr, arrived to welcome them. This was followed by a dynamic and enthusiastic telegram of welcome from Lord Beaverbrook, as the responsible Minister in London. Naturally, we had a celebration dinner. But what amused me about these brave men who had faced the real hazards of the Atlantic, was that they were terrified to go outside the hotel into the blackout. A few days later, leaving their aircraft behind, they went back across the Atlantic by boat.

On another occasion, and this shows a bit about what is happening today, two English military security men arrived from Antrim and asked to see me.

They said : "You have two men, X and Y working in the Maintenance Unit. We want them dismissed."

"Why," said I as Security Officer. "What have they done?"

"Oh nothing, but they are Roman Catholics."

"Well," I replied. "So am I. What's wrong with security there ?"

"Ah, it's different. We are told in Antrim that they come from the South."

"Well so do I," I replied and they went back not knowing quite what to think.

At that time the Army Commander in the North was General Carton de Wiart. He was a V.C., had lost an arm and an eye, but what alarmed a lot of locals was that he was a Roman Catholic. In fact, indeed, he was the only V.C. from my old School, the Oratory. I often went up to lunch with him in Ballymena.

Ulster was then, and until recently, very largely patrolled by a force of local, mostly young farmers, called "B Specials". They are a pretty tough lot, not at all enamoured of Catholics and not suffering from a great sense of humour. I was responsible for providing lectures and entertainment for those around Antrim. I managed to persuade General Carton de Wiart to come and tell them how he got away from Poland at the start of the war, where he was then living.

It did a lot of good and opened their eyes to another side of life. But at the same time I ask myself, as did Miss Devlin in her maiden speech, does anyone born English and at Whitehall really understand Ulster. Why send General Carton de Wiart to County

Antrim? Why send, the other day, the Ulster Rifles to Gibraltar where last year their Protestant wives had for months to watch their children brought up in Catholic Christian Brother schools, until the War Office provided other schools, since there were no others. And just after the war, why did Conservative Head-quarters in London send me over to a big Young Conservative Rally at the Sleeve Donard Hotel in Newcastle, Co. Down? One must not forget that, in many parts of Ulster, Catholics are not even accepted to be members of the Conservative Party Association. On that occasion a very good friend of mine, named May, now dead, who might well have made the best leader of the Unionists today, who had been stationed at Aldergrove with me, came specially to the airport to meet me and motored me down to Newcastle—quite a journey—and Lord Brookeborough, who was a most ardent Protestant Prime Minister, took the chair for me, thus ensuring that there were no incidents. They never said a word but they had thought it out. Only a couple of years ago the Conservative M.P. for North County Down, George Currie, asked me to come over and be the guest speaker at his summer rally in Mr. Andrews' (Deputy Prime Minister then) garden. Soon I got a note that they wouldn't be having a speech, but they hoped I would judge the beauty competition.

After I had been a little over a year at Aldergrove it was decided, since the R.A.F. had increased so much in Ulster, to make the whole area into a Group and to prepare for the day when the United States Air Force might move in. Half the Parliament buildings at Stormont were taken over and the whole Senate wing was turned into a full scale Operations' Room and H.Q. A new A.O.C., Air Commodore Lawson, was appointed and I was made his Personal Assistant. It was a fascinating job and I went with him all over the North and even (in civvies), down to see the lights of Dublin. The A.O.C. occupied the room of the Governor of Northern Ireland, the Duke of Abercorn, and I had a small room next door. During this time the Catholic Chaplain came to see me and pointed out that there were now quite a lot of Catholics, both male and female in our headquarters and that, as we were billetted in different requisitioned homes all over East Belfast, it was awfully difficult for him to make sure that they went to mass on Sundays; he calculated that there were about forty of them and he wanted to find somewhere central to say Mass. Not thinking of any serious consequences I immediately suggested the Governor's room, which I knew the A.O.C. would not need on a Sunday, and so for three Sundays, and for the first time in history, the Roman Catholic Mass was said in the Parliament buildings of Stormont.

Naturally, this was published in the usual Orders of the Day. The Military Liaison Officer serving with us was the M.P. for Derry, Sir Ronald Ross. He came to me and said, "Willy, are you mad? Don't you realise that Carson is buried just under the Governor's window? He'd turn in his grave!" What happened afterwards I do not know, but within a month I had been posted back to Fighter Command.

Just before then, the A.O.C. told me that Air Marshal Sir Richard Peck was coming over to the far north near Derry. He himself did not want to go there, he was too busy, and so would I go and represent him? I did. The Air Marshal had known me since I was at Oxford, whilst he and his great friend, Sir John Slessor were young Squadron Leaders. He asked me what on earth I was doing. I told him that I had volunteered because I knew Japan fairly well and had been sent over to Northern Ireland, where I seemed to have come to a dead end. Partially due to this I was posted back to Fighter Command and then to his department at the Air Ministry.

So much for my period in Northern Ireland during the war. I might be writing about the position as it is today. Things have in recent years got steadily worse, but the background remains almost the same. I go almost every year to both Northern Ireland and the Irish Republic. I helped start three years ago the Anglo-Irish Committee at Westminster and when I retired in 1969 I was its Vice-Chairman. I see a good deal of the Northern Irish M.P.s at Westminster, but only one of them had the courage to join the Anglo-Irish Group. What can I say of the future— and for the whole of Ireland?

I am most pessimistic for the North over the next few years. Earlier, I have said that the real Ulsterman, be he Protestant or Catholic, does not get on too well with his Southern neighbour.

When we had the troubles in the South in the nineteen-twenties I went through it all. Those like myself, educated in England, were badly let down by Lloyd George and we never stood a chance in political life south of the border—or in diplomatic life either. Every good post there went, and still goes, to either one side or the other of those who took part in the 1916 rebellion or in the civil wars of later on, and there is still deep bitterness between the two sides. Landowners have been only tolerated; and sometimes their homes were burnt down.

It was not so in the North. The landowners there remained in control and have done so right up to this day. Captain O'Neill is, after all, a distant cousin of Major Chichester-Clark and the O'Neill's name is really Chichester—they both inherited their lands and positions through the female line and their immediate ancestors changed their names. They want to be tolerant and fair, but behind them stands the unbending Orange Order and any-one in politics who goes against this will be broken. The Paisleys may do the North much harm—but they have a very strong following. On the other side there are, in addition to Civil Rights followers, many who want to get the North back for the South. They feel that it is now or never—since the high rates of the British Social Services are tempting the workers of the North away from joining the South. Yet again in the South a tariff wall has been built up against the North, so that the businessmen of the South are not too keen on any amalgamation. Not all this, of course, is said from the public platforms, nor is it publicly admitted that the Belfast men work harder than those from the South and could, given an amalgamation, probably put most people in the South out of business. Nearly everyone knows this. But then, to bedevil everything, you have the idealism of the Irish and the long memories.

To keep things as they are in the North—I mean the *status quo*—may well mean that the U.K. will have to put in more troops and then the stately homes of the North which were un-touched when those of the South belonging to "the Ascendancy" were burnt to the ground in the early nineteen-twenties, may go the same way as those did in the South. We may yet be in for very worrying times and whether the solid phalanx of Ulster

Unionist M.P.s at Westminster will be returned at the next Election to help the Tories is in no way certain.

I foresee great bitterness if either Mr. Wilson or Mr. Heath try to interfere too much in Ulster. Yet I am sure that there is toleration below the surface. When I married in 1942 the eldest sister of Ireland's senior Chieftain, O'Conor Don, who is himself a Jesuit Priest, Cosgrave, an Irish Prime Minister, came to the wedding and the President of Ireland, Dr. Douglas Hyde who was a Protestant, but crippled, made my wife and I motor from our wedding reception at Lucan House to his official residence in all our wedding garments to drink champagne with him. Several politicians suggested that one day she and I might inherit his position.

Still all this shows that there is an undercurrent of tolerance about. But anything might go wrong. It is in this spirit that I have my own suggestion to make, bred out of my many years experience of the problem.

When we were discussing the Reform of the House of Lords, largely due to Anthony Wedgwood-Benn, not only came up the question of the Scottish peers, but the Irish peers also woke up to their claims and their rightful grievances. From then on some of us have been trying to get them back into the Lords where they rightly belong. It could be a great help towards uniting us once again in some form with North and South Ireland.

Lord Robert Grosvenor, now Duke of Westminster, and myself brought this up in the Commons. Lord Sandwich (now Victor Montagu) did the same in the Lords but so far we have not had any success. We have formed an Irish Peers' Association with Lord Dunboyne and the Earl of Bandon, the Earl of Antrim and Lord Farnham as its leaders and I have offered to take over the Honorary Secretaryship. We are now fighting the Ombudsman; Lord Rathcavan wants to help us, but only if the Peers are from Ulster. The Treaty giving us the twenty-eight seats was however, between the Monarch and his Peers of Ireland and has never been revoked, and has nothing to do with coming from Ireland. Even Lord Curzon was made an Irish Peer when he went to India.

For fifty years the gerrymandering which got rid of three of the counties of Ulster and left them to the South, because their majorities would have been Nationalist, made the Six Counties of Northern Ireland "safe" at least temporarily for the Unionists—but they have not been tolerant enough to their quite considerable minority and at last rebellion has erupted. The British Home Secretary, Callaghan, has shown real statesmanship. He has completely outshone the Stormont politicians who, in reality, are mostly little more than glorified Town Councillors with little or no real political knowledge.

To my mind the Constitution giving Stormont internal control is now dead, but it will take time to bury it.

As far back as 1795 (and we always think back a long way in Ireland) there were in Armagh two big groups: "The Peep o'Day Boys" and the Defenders. "The Peep o'Day Boys" were so called because they came just before dawn to the homes of the Catholics before anyone was up and took away their guns and their arms. The Lieutenant of the county of Armagh, the Lord Gosford of those days, gives a terrifying description of how these people—the originators of the Orange Order who, however, are not as many think, Freemasons—tried to exterminate not only the Catholics but to a lesser extent the Nonconformists of his county, all loosely called the Defenders.

My great-grandfather, then seventeen, just after the battle of Diamond Hill, son of the leading Catholic in Lisburn, went into Armagh to try and bring about peace, but unsuccessfully. He then collected Mr. Neilson, another influential Catholic, and they went again. The whole story is told by him, Charles Teeling, in a pamphlet on Diamond Hill, which the Dictionary of National Biography describes as: "the best report on the start of the Orange Order from a Catholic point of view extant".

My family have followed the problem to this day. We were always for a United Ireland, but not necessarily independent. I still feel that Ulster is necessary to be in a united Ireland for the health of the whole nation and I believe that, after a time, the whole United Ireland, possibly in a United Europe, would be so linked up with our Commonwealth in such a manner that all today's horrifying happenings could be forgotten. But after all this bitterness it must take time to be achieved.

The smallest reform I would insist on is the banning of bands, processions and the beating of the Orange drums. It seems, somehow, that nothing can happen in the North without people rushing to get a band and soon they are carried away by the martial music. It's silly, but it's a fact—it's like the bagpipes for the Highlander; and Scotland and Ulster have much the same background.

I think that the housing question has rightly been taken out of the hands of too narrow-minded locals and I feel that Stormont has been tried and found wanting, largely because of secret societies and the Orange Order. But none of this for years will get rid of the deep down mistrust started in 1795, of both Catholics for Protestants and vice versa. After all, the Protestants know that their majority in the six counties is diminishing and it terrifies them.

Why should we not have a solution something on the lines of what Julian Amery in the six months he spent in Cyprus as Minister of State for the Colonies, worked out for Cyprus? Why not leave a small area around Harland and Wolfe's dockyard and as far afield as Larne (like at Famagusta and Limassol), where the U.K. would be allowed to be in control of everything? The U.K. after all, needs a little bit of Ireland for its own defence purposes and the workers there and all over Ireland would then have that bit secure for industry, as had Malta until recently. The economy would be helped and I believe that such a small area is all that can peacefully be left from the present wreckage. In the end the Catholics must from sheer numbers prevail, but they are not really I.R.A's at heart, nor even really Labour (Morrison always hated the Irish Labour leaders), but what will be the effect of Quintin Hogg's speech at the Brighton Conference 1969 nobody can tell.

* * *

When I was posted back from Northern Ireland and joined Lord Stansgate and Lord Willoughby de Broke in the Public Relations side at the Air Ministry (after a short spell at Fighter Command) as liaison with Air Intelligence, I had to find a home. I had sub-let my Albany Chambers on joining the R.A.F. Lady

Betty Baldwin, who was doing W.V.S. work came to my rescue
and found out that Natalie Hogg, afterwards Madame Coulet,
was having some difficulty with her father-in-law, Lord Hailsham,
in justifying keeping on a house in Victoria Square. She and
Quintin Hogg had no children; she was in the A.T.S. I think at
Aldershot, and Quintin (then M.P. for Oxford City) was in the
Middle East.

When she heard that I needed to be a p.g. somewhere, she
said it was just what they needed and Lord Hailsham was at least
temporarily quietened. I spent some happy weeks there and after
a bit Natalie was posted back to London. The sister of Mrs.
Liddel-Hart, she was a handsome woman of considerable intelligence and I would have thought of considerable use to Quintin.
Later, it turned out that she fell in love with one of De Gaulle's
right-hand-men, M. Coulet. Quintin divorced her and she married Coulet. At the Normandy landings De Gaulle put him in
charge of all the civil side of Normandy life in spite of the
Americans and later he was offered the Embassy in Delhi, but
the Indians would not have him as his wife had previously been
married to a prominent British M.P. Instead he became Ambassador to Persia and afterwards to Portugal, Natalie being a most
decorative Ambassadress; I believe she was French-Canadian.

Very soon after, Quintin married Miss Martin, not only from
the West of Ireland but a cousin of the Miss Martin of Ross, who
always wrote with her cousin Miss Somerville, as "Martin Ross"
(their most famous book being *The Tales of an Irish R.M.*).
Quintin has now a large family and is immensely happy. When
the first Hogg menage began to break up I moved in as p.g. to
Lady Betty Baldwin in Grosvenor Square where I was very well
looked after.

CHAPTER VII

YALTA AND SERBIA (MIHAILOVITCH)

O N THE morning of 8 February 1944, Anthony Marlowe, in Colonel's uniform, collected me at Brooks's Club in Flight Lieutenant's uniform; we entered a taxi and I was thrilled to hear the remark: "House of Commons please; Members' Entrance." On arrival we reported straight to the Government Chief Whip (James Stuart) who with Tony Marlowe, my fellow Member now for Brighton, was to introduce me to the House. We went up and down the Aye Lobby practising the procedure and then I ran into Jock MacEwen, the only Catholic Whip and a convert at that, which is supposed to make one more zealous. He reminded me that when I was offered the Bible on which to take the Oath, I must ask for the Douai Version which is the Roman Catholic one. Until quite recently R.C.s and others, except of course Jews or those who would only attest, had taken it on the official Church of England Bible. But Dick Stokes, also a Catholic, kicked up a fuss and finally got Speaker Fitzroy to buy a Catholic version for our use.

In a way I am glad that I got into the tail end of the 1935 Parliament, but it was not an easy one in which to find one's way about. To begin with, the House of Commons had been completely bombed out and we, the Commons, had taken over the House of Lords.

This latter chamber had been switched round and the Throne removed. It was not thought right that the Speaker should sit where the Monarch had sat before and so his Chair was placed facing where the Throne had been at the other end of the Chamber. The Lords moved in to what is now, and was previously, the Robing Room. It was therefore in the House of Lords that I made my maiden speech and probably the only speech that I will ever make in that Chamber. Only a few weeks after I had made it, the "doodle bombs" and the V2s began to come over London and it was considered that there was too much glass in the buildings at Westminster for it to be safe. We moved secretly into what today is Church House where the Church of England Assembly meetings take place.

The last few weeks at Westminster certainly became exciting; as I was also fire-watching at night on the roof of Westminster Abbey it became a little too exciting.

While we sat upstairs in Committee the bombs could often be heard coming over and all of us ducked—we had the ordinary sort of school desks and we got under them. I used to wonder why it always took the rather elderly and fat Admiral Sir Murray Sueter, so long to get down; he turned around and always went down head foremost. I had the cheek to ask the reason why. He told me that his wife had made him promise to do that, so that if there was any splintered glass, his face would be protected and it would only go into his exposed posterior; and it was a big one too. He looked very funny.

The social life in the Commons in those days was almost non-existent and, as a new boy, you missed it very much. The Whips, especially the senior ones, were far too busy with the Government to bother about one new by-election product, except for Jock MacEwen. He, although not my official Whip, was the only one to take some trouble and give me some advice : "Don't make your maiden speech too soon" was one piece of advice I took, unlike my compatriot Miss Devlin later on. "When voting, if you are in any doubt, give the benefit to your Party's official line" was another—though not always, since more than once I was in no doubt at all that the Party was wrong. I voted against the Party line, first on Yalta and later on on Lend-Lease, the evacuation of Suez in the early 'fifties, and again over the Suez debacle, over Resale Price Maintenance, over Rhodesia, and indeed over much else.

Paddy Hannon advised me to specialise in one subject and not get a reputation for talking too much or for knowing just a little about too many subjects. I decided to specialise on Foreign Affairs especially Far Eastern affairs and later on over the repayment of debts owed us from abroad; on the Channel Tunnel and, while the problem lasted, on Malta.

I remember being rather pleasantly taken aback when I came up from the Dining Room one evening and asked the Whip, Peter Agnew, what this particular Division was about—to which he replied: "I haven't the faintest idea, but I know it's landlords to the right!" Charles Howard-Bury, an ex-M.P., advised me to sit in a lot at Question Time: "It will make you get to know who different people are, as it's really the only time their names are called out before they rise." Tom Driberg said: "Don't make your maiden speech till you have asked a few Questions and so have gotten the pitch of the Chamber," and Paddy Hannon again said: "Tip a lot and everywhere—the Staff and Police can help you a lot." As a result, many a time a telephone call to my Club saved me from missing a Division.

Later on when I had been asking a lot of Questions and getting rather dusty Answers from both Churchill and Eden, my old friend Oliver Stanley who had more or less sponsored me, with his wife, for Bury, sent for me and in the nicest way said: "They don't mind the Questions you ask, so much as they resent the way you put them." This was the first friendly hint I got as to where I was going wrong. Another came from J. P. L. (Jim) Thomas, who told me that, when I got in, naturally many people who had never come across me wanted to know what I was like.

As I planned to use such experience as I had obtained abroad, I felt that I had better make my maiden speech in a Foreign Affairs debate. I asked one or two friends for points that might be helpful, one of them being Air Marshal Sir Richard Peck, my Air Ministry boss. His two interesting comments were: "We are fighting for democracy, but we will only win if we are rather unscrupulous about ignoring democracy, to win our objective," and the other: "Rub into M.P.s that we should never have won the Battle of Britain had it not been for two badly-needed extra Squadrons which were all Polish; and the Poles over this war are more prepared to commit suicide than anybody else is, except the Japanese."

7.   The Regency Ball in Brighton, 1946.

Left to Right: Ratu Edward Thakumbau of Fiji, Mrs. Teeling, the Author, Sir Anthony Tichborne, Bt., Mr. George Ritchie.

8. The Author and other M.P.s visiting a film studio near London.
Left to Right: Col. Sir Tufton Beamish, M.P., the Author, Roland Robinson, M.P. (now Lord Mantonmere), Stewart Granger, Douglas Dodds-Parker, M.P.

It is true that, if the Battle of Britain saved us and the war, it was the Poles who saved the Battle of Britain—which brings me to my first rebellion over the Yalta Agreement when, within about a year of being elected, I deliberately voted on a Vote of Confidence, against Churchill over Yalta. Nothing was said from the Whips' Office but there was certainly trouble in Brighton (mostly in the Hove end). There were still many people angry at my election and they had a special meeting called of the Executive where I had to explain my position. I was given a unanimous vote of confidence.

Perhaps I was not cynical enough after only twelve months in Parliament to avoid being horrified by Churchill's and Eden's attitude to the Polish claims.

As recently as 1968, when the Russians invaded Czechoslovakia. General De Gaulle and most of France stated that all this invasion was due to Yalta; Americans are saying today that Roosevelt was too ill at the time.

What was our attitude? Churchill tried to justify everything in the debate in the Commons on February 27th and 28th, 1945. If Churchill had said, as Maurice Petherick in moving the Amendment against the Government pointed out, that he had reluctantly agreed to what Stalin had insisted, in spite of our definite promise to Poland in the past, some would have understood. But that Churchill should blatantly defend the Russian attitude; say that it was right that we should go back to the old Curzon line; give Poland (if we had the power to do so) vast areas of East Prussia and Silesia in return for taking from her her right to vote freely on this matter; and that Eden should do so too, when he already knew as far back as September, 1944, that, since Russia occupied part of Poland in one district alone near Lublin 21,000 Officers and men of the home army had been placed under arrest, and how General Bor and his underground forces were being accused of being pro-Nazis; this seemed to me too much.

Maurice Petherick informed us that what Churchill had agreed to would mean that Poland, now over-run by Communist Russia, would lose nearly half her present territory, a third of her population, 85 per cent of her oil and natural gas, half her timber and peat, half her chemical industry, nearly half her grain, hemp and

G

flax, and nearly 40 per cent of her water power, potassium mines and phosphates and the ancient city of Lvov. I was horrified to hear Churchill tell us about these Agreements at Yalta, then calmly admit that he had not even consulted the Polish Government in exile in London, or even brought their representatives to Yalta—though the Lublin puppet government of the Russians had representatives there. He added rather petulantly "that had the Government in exile gone back to Poland last year, as he had suggested, they would now have control". I would have thought that they would all have been sent to Siberia! During the year I had been in Parliament I had seen a lot of the Poles in exile— they had a rehabilitation Home in Brighton. I knew something as well of what was happening in Poland. I could not believe that Churchill, after all our Treaties with the Poles, could speak as he did.

My mind went back to only a few months before, when in the Smoking Room he had spoken to me very impatiently about the obstinacy of the Poles, and that he would not let them come between him and Russia. The war must be won with Russia's help and then, and then only, we could turn to other smaller-State problems. Churchill was certainly looking at everything from one angle only—British victory—and we cannot blame him. But why he never even consulted the Government he recognised, and how, with all the knowledge in his hands, he dared get up and say that he was sure Poland would have free elections, to this day I cannot understand. Lastly, when he referred to the Polish forces, over 200,000 of them under that wonderful man, General Anders, who were outside Poland and fighting closely with us, in the same tone of arrogance as he used in offering British joint nationality to France in 1940, which had so infuriated many of the French; and now made the same offer to these Poles outside Poland, I could not vote with him. I thought back to all the Poles who had been to school with me or at Oxford with me. What proud and quixotic people they were! How could he expect them to accept it? I opposed him and he did not forget it.

Go any Sunday even now to a Polish Mass at the Brompton Oratory or elsewhere; it must make you feel sad and ashamed to see the proud poverty of those who remain, old now and hopeless; and the Generals and officers living on a pittance and refused by our Treasury the pensions and the disablement benefits which they should have shared with us equally. There are many people to blame, not only Churchill, but I think that I must include a letter from Churchill which I received in the next Parliament in October 1945.

I had written to Hector McNeil, the Number Two at the Foreign Office under Ernest Bevin (4 October 1945), pointing out what Churchill had, as far as I could hear, promised, or offered, on 27 February to the Polish Forces in exile, and I wanted to follow it up. Mr. McNeil replied that this was not a pledge but a promise to investigate the possibility in special cases and that no declaration could be made until ways and means had been investigated, and ended : "Indeed we feel strongly that it would be a mistake and unfair to the Poles to ask them in the present uncertain situation, to renounce all opportunity of returning to Poland in favour of a future in exile about which His Majesty's Government can give them no certain guarantee." (My underlines.)

The actual statement of Churchill had been : "In any event H.M.G. will never forget the debt they owe to the Polish troops who have served them so valiantly; and to all those who have fought under our command I earnestly hope it may be possible to offer the citizenship and freedom of the British Empire if they so desire. I am not able to make a declaration on that subject today, because all matters affecting citizenship require to be discussed between this country and the Dominions, and that takes time."

"But, so far as we are concerned, we should think it an honour to have such faithful and valiant warriors dwelling among us as if they were men of our own blood." (My underlining.) With that, Winston sat down—it was the end of his speech on Yalta which was broadcast to the world. I did not think that the Poles would accept it—but it seemed to me the nearest thing to a pledge I could think of and certainly something he would make efforts to obtain.

I sent McNeil's letter on to Churchill and was very depressed to receive the following reply :

> 28, Hyde Park Gate,
> London, S.W.7.
> October 18th 1945

Dear Flight Lieutenant Teeling,

Thank you for your letter and its enclosure which I return.

I have looked up what I actually said in the House on February 27th and there are undoubtedly some loop-holes in my declaration, of which the Government seem inclined to take advantage. I do not propose to take any action myself.

> Yours very sincerely,
> WINSTON S. CHURCHILL.

Poor Poles; no one really cared; the war was over. There was, however, one M.P. quite recently dead, Professor Savory of Belfast University who fought for them to the end.

On the night I retired from the Commons in 1969, I went to see the play *Soldiers*, all about General Sikorski and his death in Gibraltar. I had heard that it was a violent attack on Churchill and suggested that he planned Sikorski's death. How this got about I often wonder. Nowhere in the play could I see any such suggestion; but everything Churchill was made to say in the play was what I had heard him say more than once. He would not let Poland cause ill-feeling between Russia and the U.K. and he would not let the horrible murder of brave Poles recently discovered be the cause of further ill-feeling. I still do not agree with Churchill, but I admit that there was a perfectly sound argument in his favour. But to stoop to assassination I neither believe, nor is it even suggested in the play. What one can come away thinking of is the story of Henry II and Thomas à Becket, where the King in a fit of rage shouted : "Will no one rid me of this interfering prelate?" Maybe there were others, who surmised not only how Churchill felt, but thought that the end justified the means. Knowing of the danger to Anglo-Russian relations of Sikorski obstinately standing up for Polish rights, no matter what the cost, they decided an accident was the simplest solution. Who they might be I have no idea. It is a pity that we have never been allowed to see the full report of that crash at Gibraltar. Everyone knows that it exists—why is it not published to settle everything once and for all?

Several M.P.s have attempted to put down Questions on this subject but the Clerks at the Table who are responsible for letting Questions through—it is called "Getting past the Table"—will not allow one. It was the last Question I tried to put down before retiring and goodness knows how often I have been frustrated trying to get past the rules of the House for Questions. The reply the Clerks gave me was that the Government is not responsible for the decisions of previous Governments, nor for what they have decided to do (the previous Governments) about publishing reports of enquiries they have made.

In August 1969, a correspondence developed in *The Times* on whether Hitler should have been shot out of hand from the windows of the flat in Berlin of the then British Military Attaché in 1938. The latter wanted to do this and also later planned various unconventional actions which showed that, if someone was doing Britain any damage, he felt that all means would be fair to be rid of him, even if it meant others having to die as well. This was Noel Mason-Macfarlane. He later headed a military mission in Russia up to and during 1942, and I'm told he loathed the Communists. In 1942 he became Governor and Commander-in-Chief in Gibraltar and remained there until 1944; which means that he was Governor when Sikorski met his death there. In 1944 I believe he quarrelled with Churchill and by 1945 he had left the Army and joined the Labour Party and I remember him well in his high-necked jumper taking the oath as M.P. for North Paddington. He was, however, already a dying man and retired in 1946 to die in 1953. It would be interesting to know what he really knew or felt about Sikorski's death.

About the same time as this correspondence appeared in *The Times*, there was published a French book which sold well in Paris, about the death of Sikorski and written by David Irving. In this book the author stressed General Mason-Macfarlane's great appreciation of Sikorski and his hospitality to him on the day of Sikorski's death. He also points out that Sikorski's widow would not attend the Victory Parade at Churchill's invitation in 1945.

The only Minister of our Government who went really out of his way to try and help the exiled Polish Forces after the War was Harold Macmillan and he backed appeals for them organised by Lord Astor and Lord St. Oswald.

Shortly after the Profumo Scandal, I remember Bill Astor who had figured prominently in the publicity about the parties at his place, Cliveden, telling me how he was called to 10, Downing Street to see Macmillan about the appeal for the Polish retired Generals and Colonels. He had quite a long session with the Prime Minister whilst a Cabinet meeting was due. The members of the Cabinet were kept waiting and when the door eventually opened and out came Lord Astor there was a look of horror on some of their faces. They thought that a new episode in the Profumo problem was about to start. Astor reassured them.

In passing, I would say that the rules about Questions are amongst the most important of the many things which need reform in the Commons. How far we are still governed by that Bible of Parliamentary procedure produced by the late Lord Farnborough—better known as Erskine May—in regard to Parliamentary Questions I do not know: but, in the last twenty-five years, we have certainly found it more and more difficult to get Questions past the Chair and yet they are as strong a safeguard for the liberty of the subject as any of our Parliamentary customs.

The constant quotations from Erskine May by different speakers, which frustrate everybody since they seem to be uncontradictable, have tempted me to find out who he was and when he lived.

It seems that he was Clerk of the House of Commons from 1871 to 1886. He was the first person to put down in writing The Rules, Orders and Forms of Procedure in the House of Commons and, as nobody questioned him they were printed by Order of Parliament and were translated into German, French, Italian, Spanish, Japanese and Hungarian. He was made a Peer as Lord Farnborough on the 10th May 1886 and died one week later. He has a window dedicated to his memory in St. Margaret's, Westminster.

However, back to my first Parliament. During those last eighteen months of that Parliament of the War years—I got involved still further in trouble with Churchill and Eden over foreign affairs. This time it was about Yugoslavia and Mihailovitch—a tragedy which is perhaps half-forgotten today, but which should always be remembered.

Mihailovitch was to Serbia what De Gaulle was before the war to France, a brilliant strategist and a great and fearless soldier. Mihailovitch was a loyal follower of the Monarchy, and a Serb, as distinct from the Croats and the rest of Yugoslavia. He was a member of King Peter's Government right up to 1944; but he stayed on in Yugoslavia at great risk, and in the first two years of the war did such brilliant sabotage of the German forces with his 200,000 men, called the *Chetniks*, that he received telegrams of congratulation on his successes from General Eisenhower, Field Marshal Auchinleck and Air Marshal Tedder. But he was not a Communist and he did not like Tito and the Partisans.

What happened next? Suddenly, in May 1944 Tito's representative, General Velebit, came to London; and our liaison officers with Mihailovitch were withdrawn. A campaign of vilification against Mihailovitch was started in the Press and on the wireless. Members of the Serbian Government came to see me about it and I put down a Question for 17 May that year. Even I did not then know how our Government was rapidly switching over to Tito. Eden was very evasive; a few, but only a few, M.P.s on my side backed me then; I asked for the Adjournment. It took me until 20 June, another month, to get it. Slowly the story of what was going on in Yugoslavia began to come out. Mihailovitch fought bravely for the Allies—but every bridge or railway line he sabotaged, was rebuilt by the Germans in a few weeks. In the meantime the Germans took reprisals on the nearby villages. The *Chetniks* had swooped down from the hills to cause their havoc and went quickly back again; but the villagers were always there.

The Germans cleverly took reprisals on the well-to-do of the villagers and burnt and looted their farms. Knowing that the *Chetniks* were on King Peter's side, they left his enemies, the Tito Partisan supporters or the Communists alone, saying that these were not responsible. After a time Mihailovitch began to realise that this was weakening his support in the country and benefiting the Communists.

He sent messages to Churchill and to the U.S.A. to say that he was not prepared to go on unless the Allies assured him that they would land and invade. This they would not do. Churchill wanted to, I always understood, but the Americans preferred to come up through Italy and the South of France. Mihailovitch refused to continue what he considered was a massacre of his people to no real purpose. Again the old story; he was looking ahead to his country's future and that it should not be Communist; whereas Churchill was only thinking of harassing Germany and always told us that he trusted Russia.

Shortly after this unsatisfactory Adjournment debate which George Hall (afterwards First Lord of the Admiralty in the Labour Government and then Viscount Hall), conducted with pious platitudes I began to obtain more evidence.

By 7 July I was back on the warpath again. This time I tackled Brendan Bracken, the Minister of Information, on what was being broadcast to Yugoslavia. Bracken's family background in Ireland I knew well. As a young man back from Australia I saw him make good in London. He was the type Churchill liked—clever and ruthless. We were telling the Yugoslavs that their King had dismissed his Government actually one week before he did so. Churchill did this, no doubt misinformed, but Bracken knew it well. Evidently we were determined to go all out for Tito and Eden asked me to go and see our Ambassador to Yugoslavia.

He was, it seemed, to persuade me that I was wrong. Alas he did not, any more than he persuaded me three years later that he was right in his advice in his new post in China where I ran into him again. We have always, I think, remained good friends, but he never convinced me and the fact that Eden put such trust in his advice frightened me. During this bitter debate on Yugoslavia, Bracken was pretty sweeping in the things he said and a well-known authority on that part of the world whom I quoted, Voigt of "The Nineteenth Century and After", later sued for libel one of the M.P.s who spoke in support of Bracken and got quite substantial damages. There was much bitterness at that time amongst the refugee governments in London. Bracken was definitely "His Master's Voice" for Churchill over Poland, Yalta, Sikorski, Serbia and elsewhere.

Brendan Bracken who was Mr. Churchill's Minister of Information during a large part of the War, always seems a mysterious character to the British, but certainly not to the Irish. Perhaps the "Ascendancy Class" in Ireland did not know much about him, but I understand that this may well be cleared up, and high time too, by a book about him from the more Catholic side of Ireland.

He was born about 1901 and was one of a fairly large Catholic family from Tipperary. He was distinctly a thorn in his family's side, a "problem child" and was expelled at least five times from Irish schools—quite a record! By the time he was fourteen his family had had enough of him and they sent him out to relatives in Australia. There he earned a living by teaching and got enough together to get back to England. It was later pretended that his Australian relative had left him a fortune.

He next continued to teach in Liverpool and earned enough to get himself into Sedbergh—at the age of nineteen though he said he was only sixteen. By this time all his Catholicism had more or less been dropped, but he moved in to London and interested himself in financial papers, at which he made quite a success.

About 1925 or 1926 I used to run into him monopolising all the conversation at parties of the "bright young things" and the slightly aesthetic rather smart groups. He soon met Winston Churchill who took to him and found him useful and he never looked back. His father was mixed up with the Gaelic Athletic Association and was almost certainly a Fenian. Most of them were, and the precursors of the I.R.A. His nephew, a Jesuit, was a contemporary of my brother-in-law (also a Jesuit). Bracken was certainly not the sort of person to have any sympathy with my monarchist friends of Yugoslavia—but ready to do anything Churchill wanted doing and to fight Churchill's enemies, Poles or Yugoslavs.

He never talked about Ireland to me (though he was aware that my relatives knew most of his background), until the day he saw in *Country Life* that I was selling my home at Lucan, near Dublin. He showed that he knew it quite well and knew too that Dick Stokes the Labour Minister of Works was thinking of buying it as a future British Embassy—but agreed with me that as the birthplace of Patrick Sarsfield who was defeated by William III at the Battle of the Boyne, it would be probably burnt down if the British took it over. It is today the Italian Embassy. Never before and never again did Brendan Bracken speak to me of his Irish links. He preferred to be known in Westminster as starting at Sedbergh and he built up quite a legend about his really rather unromantic past.

About that time I was lunching next to Clare Sheridan, Churchill's first cousin. She told me that she was writing a book about her American ancestors, the Jeromes. In it she shows how her grandfather (also Lady Randolph Churchill's father) had married a Miss Clara Hall, a quarter Iroquois-Indian, who in turn had a Red Indian grandmother, the wife of David Wilcox of Williamstown.

"Winston," she said, "asked me not to mention this until the war was over as he had enough difficulty already with the Americans without showing that his great-grandmother was half Red Indian.

The high cheek-bones of the Red Indians are quite noticeable in some of the Jerome descendants.

Earlier on I mentioned that General De Gaulle and the French Radio in 1968, laid the blame for what is happening now in Eastern and Central Europe on the decisions of Yalta. Captain Alan Graham, Selwyn Lloyds' predecessor as M.P. for the Wirral, mentioned in his speech in the debate on Yalta, how odd it was that France had neither been consulted, nor even mentioned. De Gaulle never forgave that insult and we are paying for it dearly these last few years. When I left the House of Commons in 1969, I was the last remaining M.P. who had voted against Yalta and I was, I think, the last M.P. to speak up for Serbia when she too was handed over to the Communists.

I want to jump for a minute into the Parliament of 1945/50 with its vast Labour majority. It was only three months old when we discovered that, just before a typically Communist-type of General Election in Yugoslavia, Tito had invited out no less than eleven Labour M.P.s from Westminster to "see for themselves how the election was carried out". I raised the matter on the Adjournment and got an hour and ten minutes' debate, which I hoped would put paid to the claim in Yugoslavia that these eleven M.P.s were showing the support of Britain for Tito's Party.

I doubt, however, that I had any success. The party—whom most people called a delegation—was led by a well-known Left-wing Labour M.P., Platts-Mills, and I gather the eleven were collected by another, Mr. Zilliacus. This time I had far more supporters. But for Mihailovitch it was now too late; Tito having won his victory, Mihailovitch was tried and shot early in July 1946. I went specially to see Ernest Bevin, then Foreign Secretary at the Foreign Office. I have never seen him so deeply moved. He knew well what Mihailovitch had done for the Allies.

Just before the end, Eden asked Bevin a Private Notice Question: "Whether in view of the fact that General Mihailovitch was the first to wage guerilla warfare against the enemy and that H.M.G. supported him for over two years in this struggle, they will now request the Yugoslav Government to take his services during this period into consideration, in connection with the death sentence imposed upon him." If only a year previously he had made a statement even faintly similar!

Bevin replied: "His Majesty's representative in Belgrade communicated to the Yugoslav Government on 18 May evidence drawn up by five British liaison officers who served with Mihailovitch up till May 1944 showing that, in their experience, he actively fought against the enemy. The evidence was published in the British Press but it seemed that it was not communicated to the Court in Belgrade."

I then intervened: "In view of the fact that according to Yugoslav law, General Mihailovitch will have to be executed in 48 hours, will the Right Hon. Gentleman make sure that these reports, which appeared in the British Press, and which he said did not reach the Court in Yugoslavia, will through our British Minister, reach them before the 48 hours are over?"

Mr. Bevin: "I think that has been done."

I should (remembering our B.B.C. attacks on him a year before) no doubt have added : "And will the B.B.C. broadcast them to all Yugoslavia ?"

But it was too late.

A few days later I ran into one of King Peter's A.D.C.s in the St. James' Club. He brought me a book on Serbia : "a small memento of what you have done to help us."

He added : "I am going back to Belgrade tomorrow."

I replied : "But you are crazy."

"No," he said. "Look around this room, there are retired Poles, ex-Bulgarian and Roumanian Ambassadors. That is no life for me; you despise us all now and to see us hard up and retired makes you uncomfortable. I prefer to go back and be poor in my own country."

I never heard of him again.

During the recent French referendum a well-known Frenchman said to me : "I was in London those last years of the War. Churchill was more and more being over-ruled by the U.S.A. He knew that much that we were doing was wrong, but the U.S.A. had the whip hand, smelt victory, hated De Gaulle and wanted to divide the world with Russia—at least, Roosevelt did."

CHAPTER VIII

END OF THE WAR PARLIAMENT

IN THE last eighteen months of our long Parliament there were not very many outstanding incidents. The one I most remember was on Education. R. A. Butler, then Minister of Education, had been defeated by one vote the day before. He had been quite furious. Sir John Anderson, the rather heavily-built Chancellor of the Exchequer, had had the lobby door closed in his face; the Speaker had called "Close the doors" at the correct moment for allowing people to get to the voting Lobby and Sir John was just a second late.

As Winston Churchill put it a day or so later: "We lost because the Chancellor of the Exchequer considered it below his dignity to break into a jog-trot." Winston, however, had a ready solution for such problems. Rab's education measure was not to be jeopardised by such an event. We were summoned by a Three Line Whip to discuss—and vote—the Clause all over again. This time it went through. Jimmie Maxton, one of the most lovable extreme Clydesiders, with his hair rather long for those days and brushed down over his right eye, but much more mellowed than of old, was making one of his usual brilliant and witty speeches, but the atmosphere was tense; Winston was glowering and Rab looked sullen. Suddenly, the Liberal Whip, Bernays, appeared at a side door of the Chamber and started signalling to his flock. One by one, led by Bill Mabane, they started to troop out.

Maxton looked annoyed and contemptuously commented in his broadest Scotch; "There they go, the Liberals, as usual going to try and make their minds up."

This was too much for Bernays; he returned to the Chamber, rose and said: "The honourable Member is quite wrong. We are

going out to make a presentation to the Member for Huddersfield
[this was Mabane] who is getting married tomorrow."

"Oh, I'm sorry," flashed back Maxton, and pointing towards
the only Liberal who had not gone out—Geoffrey Shakespeare—
"And I suppose that honourable Member is the only one who has
not subscribed."

It was the first time I saw the House dissolve in laughter after
having been so tense. It cleared the atmosphere and the vote
was won for Butler.

But there were few such occasions. A large percentage of M.P.s
were away, fighting abroad. Bernays himself was to be killed a
few weeks later. The Whips were very hesitant to issue Three Line
Whips, which meant cluttering up aircraft with returning M.P.s
when the space in them was so badly needed. There was practically no effective Opposition and Nye Bevan, Dick Stokes and
Arthur Greenwood were about the only critics Churchill had to
face. After all, there was supposed to be a Party truce and except
for Secret Sessions the House was told very little of what was
actually going on. Many M.P.s drew their salary and scarcely
bothered to turn up at all. In the Lords some peers only turned
up for a few minutes to entitle them to draw their petrol ration;
they were known as P.P.s—Petrol Peers. Often there was practically no one to be found in the Smoking Room : what today is
the basement filled with dining-rooms and the Harcourt Room for
entertaining, was then handed over to working parties doing war
work who found the basement much safer than we found the
Committee Rooms with huge glass windows upstairs.

A good half of the Commons did not see what they could do
that was in any way useful. They had all been nearly ten years
in the House and many would not stand again. For new boys
like myself it was downright disastrous. We had jobs to do in the
Forces; we hardly ever met Ministers or future Ministers, since
none of us seemed to be present at the same time. I often felt
very much out of it.

But there was in our Party at least one live group foreseeing
the post-war days and wondering what would happen if
Churchill could not be got, or the Chancellor, Sir John Anderson,
would not begin, to plan out a future. At a luncheon of the 1922

Committee after we had been defeated, Winston graphically described his feelings when he heard the results of the Election. "I had had many plans prepared for the future of Europe and for a more peaceful world. They were all dashed from my hands overnight."

But what plans had he got for social betterment at home? That's what was worrying us, the younger Members, and we reported back to those at home what the Socialists were doing in the Forces. They had their socialist-minded education officers and in the constituencies where we had packed up our organisations and sent our Agents off to do war work, they on the other hand had kept on their planners, doing war work in the daytime in their areas, but meeting regularly at night. Something must be done and we tried hard to get the Beveridge Report debated and its recommendations adopted. Churchill seemed lukewarm. We formed a group called the Tory Reform Group to study and to ginger up our leaders in the Coalition Government. Hugh Molson and Peter Thorneycroft roped me in soon after I was elected. I remember when I accepted to join, I was the fiftieth M.P. to do so. It was, of course, soon in the papers and as one day I was walking along the Front at Brighton I ran into old Lord Jessel, a wonderful diehard whose family as well as his wife's family owned whole chunks of Hove.

"My dear Teeling," he expostulated, "have you gone off your head joining such a Left-wing Group? You are the Member for Brighton and Hove."

Yet today, one would smile at this definition of a group which consisted *inter alia* of Lord Hinchingbrooke, my fellow Brighton Member, Tony Marlowe, Everard Gates, Alfred Beit and many others who were not in more recent years looked on as extreme Left-wing. Behind us was Sir Frederick Hooper, looked on as a clear and brilliant thinker.

We had an office of our own, produced pamphlets (under some difficulty) and, I hope, did a lot towards preparing for our eventual future. When the Party was defeated James Stuart, the Chief Whip, let it be known we were in such a difficult position that there was no room for splinter groups in our Party. Hugh Molson was our Chairman that year and bit by bit we drifted into nothing, as we were requested, except for an occasional dinner to keep us together. It was a great pity, because in the meantime Rab Butler was building up a sort of Bow Group of his own at Central Office who today are the best known people in the Party and who have given many a Tory a feeling that we are little different from Socialists—that had not been the idea of the Tory Reformers—we might well have done our Party good had we continued active.

But Rab was determined to win back the floating vote and to go to extreme measures to do so, which alienated a group of Tories who are only now beginning in a younger generation, through the Monday Club, to spell out real policies that are not so much Right Wing as just plain right for the country.

During all this time I was fighting to consolidate my position in Brighton. It must not be forgotten that in those days there was still a strong Liberal element in the town—the constituency was Liberal in 1910—and my by-Election opponent, Dutton Bryant, came of a well-known local Liberal family. This group had tasted blood in 1944 and considered that if they had been given another week or a fortnight they would have won the election. The question now was, would they put up the same, or another "Independent" candidate against me at the next General Election?

This at all costs I had to stop, but I did not know for certain that I had succeeded until early 1945. I did not hold public meetings, but I got a lot of M.P.s down. My flat at Brighton was a very much sought after place. No outsider was allowed into Brighton without a *permit* and the cream of our Forces were all there, or around there, preparing for "D" Day and also being allowed to relax before the ordeal in front of them. My enemies spread around that I was rushing about in a large car, wasting petrol. I had even indeed been seen in it and the number was quoted. I knew this not to be true and checked up to find that this was Monty's car; he was going around the area inspecting and preparing.

I had rented a flat in the converted house of the Sassoons in Queens Gardens, Hove. My sitting-room had been King Edward VII's bedroom—but more recently it had been owned by the solicitor in the famous "Mr. A" case, where an Indian rajah had been blackmailed. It had the most ghastly Indian furniture, but I had it on a furnished tenancy and could do nothing about it. Chips Channon often came down to stay and in his memoirs I was rather annoyed to see (no name mentioned) that he was "staying in a flat furnished in the most atrocious taste". We used to sit up at night checking up what we knew personally about the tastes of different M.P.s and generally who was likely to get in at the next Election.

Patrick Buchan-Hepburn, who had been off and on a Whip and was soon to become our Chief Whip, also came and he discussed whether Whips should take a real personal interest in M.P.s, especially new ones like myself. His feeling, I gathered, was definitely no; we should look after ourselves. Hugh Molson came and discussed the Tory Reform; Bob Boothby came and discussed his own future. He was always the biggest local success; but the more M.P.s I had down, the more I took them around, especially to the houses of my more uncertain supporters. It worked very well.

Then, of course, we had all the troops stationed around. The Grenadiers were billeted all over Hove. I got them, or most of them, made honorary members of the Union Club which was rather famous for its cellar and especially its port. One officer, an old friend of mine in the Blues, alas, used the Club by himself almost every night for dinner and soon finished off the vintage port. Tanks, armoured cars and every kind of gun were parked along the squares where normally today would be placed ordinary cars. Security forbad the drivers or anyone in charge from drinking with the house owners; they did it all the same. Then, as we were clearly nearing "D" Day, some of the better off families decided to give the Officers a "Good luck" party.

Drink was procured from goodness knows where and Mrs. Charles Wakeling was the hostess. She and her husband (who had fought hard only a few months before against me and was now my strongest ally, and was later to become Vice-Chairman of my Association) lent their house with its superb garden; but obviously not everyone could be invited and so no one was entertained under the rank of Captain. Brigadier Norman Gwatkin

H

was in charge. He plumped for the last Sunday in May for the party. It was a howling success and Mrs. Wakeling was afterwards dubbed the new Duchess of Richmond for giving the modern equivalent of the Eve of Waterloo Ball in Brussels.

A few days later I was on an Air Station in Hereford when I heard that that morning we had landed. Back in the Commons it became very tense for a few days—then after that we relaxed. In October as usual, we had the State Opening of Parliament— but it was all as usual very "hush hush" and took place in the Royal Robing Room, the King in Naval uniform and the Queen wearing a hat and blue gown. It was uncanny to hear Lord Haw Haw telling us the night after on the wireless from the Continent all about it. Earlier in the year I often used to feel a little nervous as he told us all about the Australians in Brighton and that he and his friends would be dropping something on them at the Metropole soon; they never did, but it was only a few yards from where I lived if they had. I had an arrangement with the Ministry of Information to let me know immediately there had been a raid on any part of Brighton and if I was in London I would get down by the next train and visit the scene of destruction. But towards the end of the year I felt less and less well and soon I had to go into hospital for what turned out to be two rather serious operations within five days of each other. Brighton doctors started to tell the local Tories that I might well die and that they should look for another candidate. They ignored these advices and, when I recovered, the friendship of the Brightonians was such that I realised I was safe for re-adoption.

But whilst I was ill two M.P.s were killed, one Robert Bernays and the other a great friend of mine, Jack MacNamara, the Member for Chelmsford. That was where I had gone in 1926 to gain experience at a by-Election and where I remember well I had first heard Oswald Mosley speak and had been immensely impressed.

The candidate then had been the man I knew best in Parliament before I got in, Colonel Charles Howard-Bury, who lived not far from me in the middle of Ireland in the most beautiful gem of Georgian architecture at Belvedere on a lough just outside Mullingar. I often went to Chelmsford after this and got to know most of his Association Officers. When he got fed up with politics or, as he put it "With the endless flow of unnecessary correspondence," he handed over to a friend of his, Jack MacNamara, who later on became the Colonel of the London Irish.

Perhaps it was, therefore, not unnatural that when Jack was killed some of the Executive turned to me to suggest a good successor. About that time I was sharing a house belonging to Patrick Kinross in what is commonly called Little Venice, with Brian Cook who was a publisher, his uncle being the head of Batsfords. Brian like myself, was in the Air Force, but also like me he was "chair-borne". He had been looking for a seat for some time and Chelmsford chose him. I went down to help him during the campaign, just out of hospital, and we both moved into the house of General Wigan, the President. Against Brian was standing a W/Cmdr. Millington. He, unfortunately for Brian, was very much "air-borne" as distinct from "chair-borne" and used to come back to speak and canvass direct from bombing German targets. He was representing a new Party formed by Richard Acland, called the Common Wealth Party and so avoided the All-Party truce which was agreed before his splinter group was started. He won the election, turning a large Conservative majority into an equally large Common Wealth majority.

It was a terrible shock to the local organisation but neither they, nor Central Office, would see the writing on the wall. There was the inevitable post-mortem at the 1922 Committee and I told them very clearly that it was quite wrong to blame Brian Cook, the candidate; he was as good as any we had got, but our organisation was not ready and the country, I warned, was getting restless with no worthwhile home plans being put before the electors. They would not listen and laid the blame on Brian Cook. A little later, Brian's uncle died, he inherited the firm of Batsfords and decided to change his name to Batsford. A few years later, in 1958, he entered the House as Brian Batsford, with Chelmsford long forgotten, as Member for Ealing South. He was already forty-eight, which is a bit late; yet he has done brilliantly, rising to be Deputy Chief Whip and later liaison officer with our G.L.C. majority. Luck, however, has been against him. Because of the Boundaries Commission plans his seat will soon disappear.

Here is a case where we should not stand against age. We need experienced older men today more than ever, especially if they are experienced in the Party machine. I remember going up to speak for Lord Salter at a by-Election in Ormskirk in 1951. He was then seventy. When Winston asked him to stand—and forced him on the local Selection Committee—he protested, as he told me, to Winston that he was too old.

"What do you mean 'too old'?" growled the Prime Minister, "you are younger than I am."

He had been previously a University Member. The House is all the poorer for the going of the University Members and also for the loss of the Independents who were already fading out when I got in—but Vernon Bartlett, Stephen King-Hall and many others have been a real loss to Parliament and to the country. They went soon after the Liberal Party. The country began to feel that giving votes to Liberals was a waste of time, how much more so to Independents, since they had no organisation; but they have been a greater loss than the Liberals and I cannot see them coming back. The machine crushes them.

Just after Yalta, Eden came to speak to the Lobby Correspondents. Their annual lunch is always a much-sought after invitation by M.P.s. At this luncheon Eden told us how he had attended a large banquet with Stalin during his recent visit. Everyone was more than merry, with caviar and vodka in abundance. Timoshenko and Voroshiloff, the two Marshals, were particularly advanced and one of them was sitting almost on Stalin's knee, tweeking his moustache. Stalin turned, a little sheepishly to Eden and through an interpreter said, "You know we have to humour these fellows. I suppose you have the same sort of trouble with Wavell." The idea of Wavell on Eden's knee was particularly pleasant.

Another evening, about the same time, Churchill told a few of us how interesting it had been at Yalta to see how Stalin, speaking in Russian, would throw out an idea as a sort of kite, and then wait while it was being translated to see how Roosevelt took it. If it was not too well, then Stalin would follow up quickly with something else or withdraw the idea altogether.

Again about this time I remember Sir William Beveridge whose

Beveridge Report in 1942 had caused such a stir, make his maiden speech to a packed House. A few weeks later he spoke again. This time he could be interrupted and heckled, and he was : also the Chamber was not a quarter full to listen to this great man. I went into the Smoking Room and commented on this to Oliver Stanley who was reading a paper. He answered : "Oh, that always happens here. People soon find their level. There is no one who gets into this House who is such an expert on something that there isn't someone who knows as much and can shoot him down."

I think Miss Devlin should remember this. How badly she was advised to speak the day she entered the Chamber. A few days later I was listening on the wireless in France to a French journalist commenting on her speech in the practical way a Frenchman can dissect : "She was moving and it was memorable, but she said little that was constructive or not already known. One felt she had put everything she knew into that speech and that we will not hear much more from her that will be effective."

It was early in the New Year of 1945 that Charles Taylor, M.P. for Eastbourne, who in the coming Parliament will be Father of the House, and I decided to go to France to see for ourselves what was happening. The Germans had not yet completely left the country and it was a sight never to be forgotten. We went first to Paris and Adrian Holman at our Embassy got us a large double room with bathroom at the Ritz. There was, however, no hot water and we could not use the bath. Looking out of the window we saw everyone going to work on bicycles; there was but little food.

Then I was told that a chauffeur had been sent up to Paris from Lisbon to collect the Rolls-Royce which our last Ambassador in France, Sir R. Campbell, had abandoned in Bordeaux in 1940 and which the Germans had brought back to Paris. Sir Ronald was now Ambassador in Lisbon and wanted his car back. If we liked, Charles Taylor and I could motor down with the chauffeur as far as Bordeaux (where I wanted again to see my aunt and her French husband) and with us would travel a delightful American lady, married to our First Secretary in Lisbon and just about to have a baby. We jumped at the idea and persuaded

Adrian Holman to get us permits from the Americans to do a detour through Normandy where we saw with our own eyes the destruction. That side of France had suffered very little until just before the landings in June 1944 and so it all had come to them as much more of a shock. They seemed to me to be very resentful both of the British and the Americans. We eventually reached Bordeaux and slept at the Splendide Hotel, but there was no breakfast and no coffee.

I then got hold of Jean Cruse, well-known in the wine business and at the moment aide-de-camp to the General in charge in Bordeaux. He made various arrangements for us and I, in the meantime, went off to see my relations in their fine house, 304 Boulevard President Wilson. My aunt told me what had happened to them. They were at their villa in Biarritz when the collapse came and they decided that they had better go back to Bordeaux. On arrival at the Boulevard President Wilson they were amazed to see sentries on the gate. They had much difficulty in getting through and found that Marshal Petain had taken over the house and it had become his headquarters.

He was very charming but he could not let them stay there. They were advised to go to their country place in the Médoc, the Château Ducru-Beaucaillou. This they did—but the next day some South American diplomats arrived to whom the authorities had allotted the house. Luckily, when they discovered that there were no bathrooms, they packed up and went back to Bordeaux. A day or so later the Marshal signed the capitulation on the marble table I know well at the Boulevard house. Later he left and my aunt and her husband thought it wisest to go back to Bordeaux. Within two days the Germans were there and took over the house. However, they left three or four rooms with a kitchenette to the poor owners and there they lived for the rest of the war, but quite unharmed. It was only after the Germans left, that there and all over France the massacres of so-called Petain-ists and collaborators took place and it is calculated that more middle-class people were killed off then than at the time of the French Revolution and the Terror.

Jean Cruse took Charles Taylor and me up, past his family place at Pontet Canet and right on to the tip of the Médoc. The

Germans were still there. They had not been evacuated and the Allies in their mopping up and sweep across France had left them to be watched from a distance by the F.F.I. *(Force Francaise de l'Intérieur)* Organisation. Charles and I brought the troops coffee and some other luxuries and we were both in turn made honorary captains in the F.F.I. On the way back we stopped off to visit a very old friend of England's, M. Achille Fould, a former Minister of Agriculture in Tardieu's Government, who was ill in his famous home, the Château Beychevelle.

In the evening we caught a train back to Paris, but it was hard going. The bridge over the Garonne had been blown up; we had to get permits to travel on the train and sat up all night. France was slowly recovering, but very slowly, and it was not from the German invasion that the damage was done, we must remember—but from our own, with much of which General De Gaulle did not agree and thought unnecessary.

CHAPTER IX

THE NEW PARLIAMENT, 1945

TOO MUCH has already been written about the Caretaker Government and the advent to power of Attlee, but as a new Back-bencher I just watched, more than a little amazed, first at the intrigues and almost heart attacks people were having to get the jobs vacated by Labour Ministers, in the break-up of the coalition, expecting it to be a foothold for the new Parliament; and then at the optimism of our own Party that we must be returned. Only one person near to Churchill had the courage to tell him that he faced a heavy defeat; that was his own Parliamentary Private Secretary, Sir George Harvie-Watt, and I believe that for quite a time after the results of the Election were known Churchill would not speak to him. To many of us the future seemed doubtful and I remember Norman Bower, M.P. for one of the Harrow seats, telling some of us that he had seen the itinerary for Churchill's "triumphant" tour during the coming Election and adding: "Thank God he is giving Harrow a wide berth." My wife, who had generations of politics in her blood, told me that she felt certain he would be defeated.

The tour itself was a triumph, simply because everyone everywhere knew about Churchill, but few had actually seen him. They cheered him as the Great War Leader, but few in the country saw him as a democratic peacetime leader, especially after one or two of his Election speeches, and in spite of years of war and years of service abroad for many, Britain then, as now, is more interested in Britain—just as France is in France and Germany in a united Germany. Churchill was interested in the world, in saving it, and especially in saving the Empire. Many people felt, and I noticed this in Brighton, that Attlee had in many ways saved Churchill during the war; that he had done all the unglamorous chores at home and had kept the Government functioning. They voted for Attlee; but luckily not in Brighton and there, after only 18 months as a very controversial new Member, even before the return of the large number of regular Tories who had been evacuated during the war, I was returned, against the tide, which swung wildly Labour, by a majority increased from 2,319 on 4 February 1944, to 18,265 in June 1945; and in addition it was a two-seated constituency where up to now Marlowe had been the senior Member. I changed places with him by getting 49,339 votes to his 49,026. It was always fun in two Member seats to see who became the "senior" Member. But with the excitement in the Commons over the general change, even this particular little triumph was completely missed, both for Marlowe and for myself.

I found myself literally between two stools. There was a completely new intake of M.P.s; they had largely been chosen because they had done well in the war, they were Brigadiers or Colonels, like Selwyn Lloyd, Toby Low and Anthony Head and Churchill insisted Shadow jobs were to be found for them—the bright boys of the future—whilst there were also those who had been many years in the House and had not yet obtained office, except a few in the Caretaker Government, or who had been serving abroad a good deal during the war, such as Alan Lennox-Boyd, Hugh Molson, Peter Thorneycroft and many more. Rightly, something had to be found for them as Chairmen of Committees in Opposition. I was no longer considered a "new boy"—I had been in the 1935 Parliament, but all I had achieved in the eighteen months I had been in the House had been to alienate Eden (and therefore J. P. L. Thomas); evidently, to a certain extent, R. A. Butler, since though it was his strong letter of support, plus Baldwin's help, which had finally got me Brighton, he hardly ever spoke to me again after I got in. That, of course, is politics; and if by taking a line to try to help the refugee Governments of countries I knew well, I cut my own political throat, I did not care—at least my "independence", as it was termed in Brighton, won me support there and secured my position for many years to come. I was better off than many of my friends who were swept out of Parliament and who never came back. For instance, East Ham was won by us in 1931 and I had been the candidate until a year before the Election. That too had now gone for good.

I shall never forget the opening of Parliament in 1945. The Lords, for one day, had moved back in to their own Chamber and the Commons were huddled together in what is normally a waiting passage from Westminster Hall to the Central Lobby; but it is on the site of where Parliament used to sit when Guy Fawkes meant to blow us up, and the Speaker's Chair was placed where it was in the days of James The First. Poor Churchill looked very fierce and stumped in to be loudly cheered by our rump.

We certainly looked a defeated lot. The Socialists were jubilant and sang "The Red Flag". When Clifton-Brown, our previous Speaker, was dragged forward, as is customary, to be Speaker again, he commented: "I wondered for a moment whether I was not being elected to be a Band Conductor." When we all took the Oath and shook hands with him he commented to me: "I'm glad to see a face I know." It must indeed be a terrible ordeal for a Speaker to learn everybody's name in the House.

When Parliament was opened in 1945 there were only 213 Conservatives and of these about half were "new boys". There were 393 Labour Members and there again quite half were new, so poor Speaker Clifton-Brown had to learn the names and get to know the faces of at least 300 people. As a Speaker he was weak, and seemed a rather frightened man. He did not understand the new intake at all. Mrs. Braddock particularly frightened him and when one day she stalked out of the Chamber because she thought that she had been kept waiting too long before being called, he sent after her to tell her that she would be called next. His Deputy, Major Milner, was different and told me once that he would never call anyone who kept on interrupting too much.

Butler started very soon after we were elected to form a group of the bright boys—not only in the Commons, but at Central Office where he set up a sort of "brains trust" from whom he chose people to push for future seats and to get them in, in 1950 and later 1951. The theory was, we had a hard core of Tories and these could be relied on throughout the country; we must sacrifice them a little to get a broader based policy which would bring in the floating vote. In this he was successful; even though he was greatly helped by the collapse of a lot of Labour morale towards the end of Attlee's rule.

His backroom boys gave us most of the policy we proclaim today and those who lead the Party now were at Central Office in 1945 to 1950 and joined the Commons then or later. They were Butler men, yet oddly enough the Party as a whole considered Butler so left and so uncertain that a lot of people drifted away from our Party in disgust over these years and are only now coming back. Maudling, Powell, Heath are all the 1950 intake—where have the 1945 intake gone? Yet they were presumably in Churchill's "Shadow" Cabinet preparing with Central Office the plans which brought us back. Looking at today's list of M.P.s and Peers who were in the Commons in 1945 for the first time only very few have made their name or are of any use for the future now—Nigel Birch, John Boyd-Carpenter, Hugh Fraser, Selwyn Lloyd, Ernest Marples, Derek Walker-Smith; and in the Lords, Heathcote Amory, Toby Low, Anthony Head and Freddie Erroll. It's not a very big or impressive list. One wonders why? It was, of course, the last list when candidates had still to pay for themselves and it may well be that many good men had been chosen for seats we never won—but I don't remember anything like the interest now taken by M.P.s and the Press in the choice of candidates. Winston wanted people who had done well in the war—but a Brigadier is not necessarily a good arguer with hecklers and many were so young that they knew little about anything before the war. Winston again (with his instinct to preserve the aristocracy) commented that the R.A.F. rather than the Army and the Navy was the fighting force of the future, and he was greatly disappointed that so few of the "Upper Classes" had gone into the Air Force—he forgot the Auxiliary Squadrons.

Well, here we were, distinctly a rump, and led by a leader, Churchill, who certainly was no Conservative; followed by Eden who always seemed so bored by home affairs—that it was noticeable when he made a public speech. The moment he got down to home problems he always turned to his notes and practically read his brief. Sir John Anderson was really a Civil Servant, Oliver Lyttleton had never been able to get the "hang of the House" and glossed over his good points without rubbing them in, as if he was making a statement at a Board Meeting. Oliver Stanley was the outstanding brain and debater and his early death has been a real loss to this country. We were left with Lord Woolton, a brilliantly successful businessman but more of an old Liberal Whig than a Tory, and Rab Butler who was openly after the floating vote at almost any cost. He may well have meant to get us back with that vote first and then turn to bring back the old Tory ideals, but he never got the chance. Macmillan had lost his seat, but we got him back soon at a by-election; I felt very proud to be one of those chosen to go down and speak and work for him at his by-election.

There was also, of course, Maxwell-Fyfe, afterwards Lord Kilmuir, who seemed to be given all the odd jobs to do; but the most revolutionary job he undertook was the reform of our Party rules. He started by abolishing the payment by Parliamentary Candidates of their Election expenses. This naturally pleased me. I had had to pay all the election expenses of the by-election in 1944 and again the year after at the General Election in 1945. I suppose that it was inevitable, but it has certainly meant the appearance of new types of candidate—and a new type of constituency Association. Moreover we were no longer to be allowed to subsidise our Agents and they were to get a guaranteed minimum salary. This was from now on to come out of the pockets of the local Conservatives. In a place like Brighton, then full of wealthy people, it was quite a change; they had never bothered to put their hands in their pockets before.

But from now on it meant that the Associations were the complete masters in choosing their candidates and in keeping them much more on a leash. M.P.s had lost yet more of their independence. Even Kilmuir, before he died, was to write a book (*Political Adventure*—Weidenfeld and Nicolson 1964) in which he was to express regret at the outcome of his reforms. As he puts it: "The trouble with the post 1950 situation was that many associations became more Royalist than the King, and assumed a control over their candidate which in some cases was tyrannical."

Each district produces a different grouping and not every one wants a working class candidate. Yet the days of the, possibly, dilettante M.P. were over: as indeed were very soon those of the Independent M.P.s. I remember the booming voice of the new Socialist Chancellor of the Exchequer, Dr. Dalton, in a restaurant, overheard by my stockbroker, telling a friend: "You know, my dear fellow, things are completely changed now, there are practically no gentlemen in the Commons, not even in the Conservative Party." Will the critics censure me if I say that one of the faults of Parliament and the Conservative Party today is that there are so few gentlemen left there? Bit by bit since 1945 the salaries of M.P.s have gone up. Today £3,250, less of course lots of tax, is the figure. It is, if we are to be paid, not enough anyway, but it is a lot more than many of the people who are choosing us get themselves and there is inevitable jealousy.

Opposite us in the Commons sat Attlee, Bevin, Dalton, Cripps, Nye Bevan, Herbert Morrison, Shinwell, Dick Stokes—a formidable group who, unlike the group to come in in 1966, had had all the experience of helping to run a Government during the War or of leading an informed Opposition—and they were professional politicians to boot.

They were bent on nationalisation—it was the cry on which they had got in. A few I believe thought that it was an out-of-date pre-war cry—but they set to to bring it about. As Lady Kemsley said to me: "Their great strength is that they carry out, for good or bad, what they promise." They carried it out and just as the Liberals, when they had got universal suffrage, their main *raison d'être*, had no more policy to present and have been looking for one ever since, so once Labour had thoroughly nationalised everything that they could, they are now looking round for a new policy.

Everyone, therefore, in 1945 was prepared to face up to nationalisation and everyone on the Conservative side was determined to fight it. With that huge majority there was little that we could do except talk, delay programmes, upset timetables and resist as far as possible. The Lords were put in a difficult position but Morrison got round this fairly cleverly and Lord Salisbury led our Party carefully. The first form of nationalisation we expected were the coal mines. A group of us volunteered to go off to the mines to get first-hand information. I visited Bolsover near Nottingham, the open-cast mines near Sheffield and the Kent and Monmouthshire mines as well; also Whitehaven. During this tour in the summer recess of 1954 I found a crying scandal that was very typical to my mind of how slipshod the Civil Service can be on details and how little really the average Labour Minister, at least in those days, cared about personal grievances; I refer to what were called the Bevin Boys—young men aged from eighteen to twenty-two who were either compelled to go into the mines or opted for them. But they had no champions and only a raw deal awaited them when the war was over. I took the matter up in the House, and, as one of them, Derek Agnew, wrote afterwards in a book :*

"The position had become deplorable when Flight Lieutenant Teeling, Member of Parliament for Brighton, made a brilliant [his words!] speech in the House which I am sure did much towards forcing a detailed statement from the Government and thus forestalling a general walk-out from the pits.

"Ft.-Lt. Teeling had consistently championed our cause by his Questions in Parliament, and his clear and lucid piece of oratory at Westminster must have a place in this book. It is the only time anybody, anywhere, has, to put it bluntly 'stood on his hind legs and given our grumbles an airing'. Every optant, ballotee and volunteer, whatever his politics, must be grateful to the Member for Brighton for that alone."

I wonder what has happened to all those Bevin Boys: the youngest must now be forty-two. One, at least, has come to light in Cecil King's memoirs—this is Paul Hamlyn the publisher to whom he refers.

* *Hansard* [414] Col. 1921 *et sec.*

CHAPTER X

ABROAD FOR PARLIAMENT

I THINK THAT the Minister I got on with best when we were in Opposition, probably because he was about my age, was Maurice Webb. He was Minister of Food, had been Chairman of the Parliamentary Labour Party for some years and previously on the *Sunday Express*. We often used to talk about his terrible disability (from which he eventually died), the amputation of his leg which was by now cut off from the very top so that there was nothing to which one could really hold a false leg. On several occasions it came off, especially when getting into a car, and at official functions this was most embarrassing. It was left just flapping in his trousers and short of taking off his trousers there was nothing to be done.

One day he was having an audience of the King when the latter said to him : "Mr. Webb, may I be personal? Will you tell me what it feels like to have lost a leg, because I believe I may have to lose mine?" To which Webb replied: "Well, Sir, it feels as if it were still there and sometimes in the Commons when we are very crowded for a debate and people press up against you, you feel as if your leg is going right through them, though they don't realise this. It happened to me one day when Mrs. Braddock came and sat next to me." This greatly amused the Monarch and he said : "You are sure it was Mrs. Braddock? Because I want to tell the Queen."

Poor Maurice did not stand again in 1955 and he was dead in 1956. He died, I believe, almost penniless, but he was one of the nicest people the Labour Party produced. He painted well and that gave him solace as more and more of his leg was cut off.

As soon as the 1945 Parliament settled down I began again

to speak on Foreign Affairs and particularly on the Far East. We had a debate on this on 20 August 1945. I wonder how many people bother to look up the maiden speeches of people who later on become prominent? On that day Jim Callaghan made his maiden speech and he chose, oddly enough, to speak about China and Japan. I wonder if he feels the same today or if he has mellowed; if not, woe betide the Japanese Emperor!

I followed him, also on the Far East and the moment I had finished up got another new Member to make his maiden speech, Fred Peart, now the Leader of the House. Quite an interesting collection for one day: two Labour M.P.s whose friendship I have always kept. Callaghan later decided on a special approach in his parliamentary speeches—the line of being aggressive and even rude. It worked well and gave him quite a position long before he took office. He is to my mind the nicest of the Labour leaders, not necessarily the best educated, but always very willing to learn and his aggressive manner belies him.

Just before we went out of office in 1964 Ted Heath had alienated yet another group of Conservatives and Jim, meeting me in the passage, said: "Bill, we've both been long enough in this House to know that if you alienate enough groups in your Party often enough, then you are sure to lose the next Election." I hope he remembers that advice today and warns his Cabinet friends.

Fred Peart has always been one of the natural gentlemen in the Commons. When his Party came down to Brighton for their first Party Conference after he was elected, I lent him and another Labour friend, Squadron Leader Kinghorn, my flat and they looked after it well. On another occasion, I lent it to Ernest Marples who drank up one of my best bottles of port and replaced it with something he bought at the local grocers. Considering how he developed a taste for good wine and now has his own vineyards, I was rather intrigued!

In 1947, James Stuart, the Chief Whip, asked me if I would like to go to Japan with Stanley Prescott, Tory M.P. for Darwen, and three Labour M.P.s who included the present Lord Lieutenant of Lancashire, Lord Rhodes. I was delighted, but it was at the time of our Party Conference in Brighton, so in order not to make my absence look too pointed I arranged to go out a week earlier with a goodwill delegation which Attlee was sending to visit Chiang Kai-shek, then President of the whole of China.

To send such a delegation today may sound strange, but at that time we had not forgotten that Chiang had been our ally all through the war, and our friend even before it; that nearly half the foreign-trained Naval, Military and Air Force Officers of China had been at either Sandhurst, Woolwich or at our Naval and Air Force centres, and of course we had had a delegation with Chiang in the interior of China all the war when he was being besieged by the Japanese.

Communism was now leaping ahead in alarming fashion and Attlee wanted as far as possible to help Chiang by sending such a delegation. It was not, however, a very strong one. We went by seaplane—the most civilised form of air travel I know—and stopped off in several countries. Lord Ammon led us; he was getting old. When we got to Siam he made the speech the Foreign Office had prepared for him for Burma—which did not go down very well. When we got to Bangkok, having been delayed 24 hours by hurricanes, we were charmingly greeted by the First Secretary at our Embassy to tell us that our Ambassador had given a dinner for us the night before, and he did not propose to give another, nor did he come to meet us.

This delighted the Chinese as it seemed to show that we were "losing face" and in order to rub it in a little more, the Chinese Ambassador gave a dinner for us himself, at the Chinese Centre. One of our delegates felt the heat a little and as he answered toasts from his hosts kept on saying as he finished each small glass "Great Britain wins" instead of the usual equivalent of "Good luck". It was playful, but not perhaps tactful; and one or two of the Chinese filled his glass with something a little stronger. Soon, as it was very hot, the Ambassador said that we should take off our coats; this we did, leaving some Members with rather brightly coloured braces. These they quickly slipped down too. Came a moment of toast drinking when one Member, feeling tired, just slipped under the table. We fished him up, but forgot that he had let his braces down and so he came up minus his trousers.

This story reached China long before we did. In Hong Kong

I bade farewell to my friends on the Chinese Delegation and awaited the delegation for Japan. We were to go to Tokyo first as the guests of General MacArthur, now in charge of the country for six weeks and we were to stay most of the time in the British Embassy.

Sir Alvary Gascoigne was our representative (we did not have Ambassadors yet as it was occupied territory). He looked after this I'm sure not entirely welcome invasion extraordinarily well, and made us immensely happy. I had stayed at the Embassy for weeks before the war with Sir Robert Clive and I knew my Japan fairly well. What a terrible change! The U.S.A. were very much in control—the Chinese were really not allowed in—except in Formosa (which they claimed as their own), the reason being that it was their custom when they invaded a country or won a war, that their troops should live off the inhabitants. But the Americans brought all their own food etc. with them and would not let the Chinese do otherwise. The British were only allowed a token occupation. They were not destined for Tokyo, but for the centre of the mainland where they would be less in evidence.

This in the long run was to our advantage, as the Japanese resented our presence less. But the money problem for us was very difficult. We had our own NAAFI but in order to get about we needed U.S. dollars and our Treasury gave us far too few. I forget now how much it was, but it was only a few shillings a day per head. Lady Gascoigne saved up to have enough to get her hair done well. General Gardiner, who represented Mr. Attlee directly, was famous as a golfer so he went out and beat the American Generals at golf. With the dollar proceeds he and Sir Alvary pooled their resources and went to the races every so often. They felt that they must be seen in public. Sir Alvary had, I think, a limitless supply of Scotch Whisky sent out from London—the Treasury allowed this and in this way he threw regular parties for very appreciative Americans. We had one Rolls-Royce for Sir Alvary. The chauffeur was so mad at the way we were treated that with Union Jack flying he drove faster than any other car. We were also allowed as a token that the sentries on duty outside the Emperor's Palace should be British—but they were Scots in kilts and the Japanese just thought them funny.

The day we arrived we were all invited to lunch at 12.30 p.m. with General MacArthur. We went in a procession of cars to his residence—but the gates were not open and the Union Jacks on the bonnets seemed not to impress the sentries. We were kept over ten minutes whilst telephoning for instructions went on. The Japanese, of course, noticed this "losing of face". Finally, when we arrived we had another quarter of an hour to wait for the General's arrival. I was amused to see Mrs. MacArthur go up to her husband and kiss him good morning with the respectful greeting of "General darling".

At luncheon I sat on MacArthur's left but we never got much chance of talking, since he never stopped doing so himself. He was convinced, and I am sure he was right, that continuity was essential in Japan. He therefore insisted on the Emperor remaining, though shorn of his power. He was not brought up in the Philippines as the local Governor's son without learning a good deal about Far Eastern mentality. It may be as well to remember here that, since MacArthur, no one at the top in the U.S.A. has studied so much and knows so much about the Far East as the new President Nixon. I hope that he will be listened to.

MacArthur expounded to me in some detail how since Shinto, the State religion, had now been abolished, there was no religion to teach the young and he also pointed out that American law did not allow the Americans to teach the growing children any religion in school. He felt that Christian missionaries were losing a great opportunity—but the clergy did not speak Japanese in anything like enough numbers. He wanted Catholics and Protestants not only to send out missionaries galore but also Catechists to teach. I went into this problem a little later with the Japanese Minister of Education, himself a Catholic, and his suggestion was that we should send out as many good biographies or autobiographies as possible to help in the schools. The Emperor agreed about this. Christianity it seemed had now a greater influence in Japan because, first of all, the Christians had won the war, which always influences the Japanese; and secondly because they thought a young go-ahead Man like Christ Who was dead by thirty-three and Who could undergo so much torture was infinitely preferable to an elderly fat Buddha sitting contemplating his navel! Everyone was frightened that Communism, a religion in itself, would gain control and no one was forgetting the hundreds of thousands of Japanese, at that time prisoners of the Russians, who would be indoctrinated with this teaching.

What has happened? Communism is there and it has certainly spread both in Japanese Universities and throughout the young world outside, but largely due to Chinese Communism. When I was last back in Japan in 1966 I was greatly impressed, but not favourably, by the completely mundane attitude of the Japanese to everything; money, money, money, that was all that anyone wanted to think about and the power that it brought. Much of the old Japanese good manners had gone and the young push you about as never before. Time is money and must not be wasted. It is part of the result of so little teaching of religion just after the war.

General MacArthur let me go and meet almost all my old pre-war friends. The wealthy Mitsuis were no longer wealthy—some of the proudest of the Emperor's staff were in considerable financial difficulties but one, the Emperor's Grand Chamberlain, told me a little ominously : "The Imperial Family, over seventy of them, are only to be allowed a lump sum to live on. If invested and the interest is paid out annually it will be really nothing, so the Emperor has told the Princes to treat it as a sum to last for five years. After that we will be all right again."

A prominent businessman said to me : "If only we had spent on developing business before the war, all we spent on armaments, now we would rule the world." That is why today there is such opposition to developing any armaments—the people want just as much to rule the world but through business. When R. A. Butler went out as Foreign Secretary he tried to get Japan to take her proper place in the defence of the East—but she would not and she seems today to be winning the trade war, with the U.S.A. and others looking after her defences. There is only one thing that still frightens Japan and that is the growth of her next-door neighbour, Communist China.

While in Japan we visited our own Air Force centres and I met many boys from Brighton. We called on H.M.S. *Sussex* and I undertook to arrange an appeal for the men to have sports equipment etc., sent out from the County. On my return I got Lord Leconfield, our Lord Lieutenant of Sussex, to back this appeal which was successful and the Duke of Norfolk gave a picture of Arundel to be hung on board.

From Japan half the delegation went home direct, but Stanley Prescott and I went on to Korea with General Gardiner in his private plane. We had a very unimpressive reception at Seoul and the Consul General seemed very apologetic. Then it was discovered that the Koreans thought M.P. stood for Military Police. When next day it was explained to them that we were the equivalent of Congressmen, all the red carpets were rushed out. At a reception at their Parliament it was explained to us how much they admired the British for getting out of India without needing to go, and could we not use our influence with the Americans so that they should do the same in Korea. When they were told that we were two Conservative M.P.s and not at all appreciative of what Mr. Attlee was doing over India they were still more amazed to think that two opponents of the Government could be allowed out of England! Which reminded me of a speech in the House of Commons of Winston's only a few weeks before, when debating Tito's activities he remarked: "I hear that a lady in Belgrade when she heard that I had been defeated at the elections commented: 'Oh dear, I do hope that he doesn't have to take to the hills!'" The poor Koreans were in a way right—it was not long before the Communists invaded. Almost all that I had seen of Seoul was destroyed and the Korean war was in full swing. Now, today, South Korea is leaping ahead economically and only the danger of another Communist invasion from the North worries her and everybody.

We next flew down to Shanghai; it was November 1947, and we found it in the same sort of chaos as I found in Germany in 1920. The Chinese dollar had catapulted down. You had to pay literally thousands of dollars for even a tie at the Cathay Hotel. The foreigners were in a panic and all wanted to come to an agreement with the Communists before it was too late and so save what they could, they hoped, of the vast sums invested in Shanghai business. It was the same in Canton where the Consul-General wanted at all costs to get me out to Hong Kong, fog or no fog.

Our British planes would not take me because I was a V.I.P. and there were certain risk regulations—but he found a New Zealand plane whose Captain said : "Our Government only has a majority of one, so we fly M.P.s in all conditions to get them back to vote." I got home via Hong Kong where again everyone was saying : "We must make friends with the Communists, the Kuomintang are finished," and Sir Arthur Morse, head of the Hong Kong and Shanghai Bank, whose guest I was for a week in Hong Kong, seemed to me convinced that the only way to save our interests in China was to recognise the Communists quickly—the Americans, of course, did not agree.

The mission I had been on was a Government and Opposition mission and Lord Rhodes and I reported back to Mr. Attlee. He was more than a little scathing when we told him that we had been asked by the Japanese to let them have some Trade Union experts out to teach them how we ran Trade Unions; that we had put this to the U.S.A. powers that be, and that it had been very forcefully turned down. Any Trade Union experts guiding Japan would be U.S.A. ones.

In addition to such Governmental studies, or visits, we have visits organised by the British Branch of the Inter-Parliamentary Union with funds mainly supplied by the Foreign Office. Only a few months before going to Japan I had gone on one of these expeditions to Finland. This as the senior Member I led. There were four of us; two women, Mrs. Ganley an elderly Labour Member and Mrs. Barbara Castle, a very bright thirty-five at that time. My male companion was Mr. (afterwards Lord) Pargiter. When we got to Helsinki we found that there had been a bit of a mistake. It was a parliamentary "occasion" to celebrate the granting of the vote to women in Finland forty years before. Every other country only sent women, so Pargiter and I were quite in demand; but in addition, every other country sent women M.P.s who, if possible, had been in Parliament or public life forty years before. There again we scored a point in having such a good-looking young lady as Barbara Castle to represent us. Finland had suffered heavily during the war and since then, so many refugees had had to be taken in that all well-to-do people had others billetted on them and there were no spare bedrooms to be found. The hotels were packed and Pargiter and I shared a room as did Mrs. Ganley and Mrs. Castle and the unfortunate Mrs. Castle had to bandage Mrs. Ganley's legs every night.

At the tail-end of the forties, Johnny Metcalf brilliantly organised a tour of the Bordeaux vineyards, which reminds me of a touching story of one of the most colourful Socialist M.P.s of recent times, Sidney Silverman. The six M.P.s and their wives were sitting in the Church at St. Emilion attending a service for the vendange; Sidney was just in front of me during the Service. The Curé was eloquent in French. Sidney did not understand it. Then came the collection. Sidney turned to me and said: "Did he say anything against the Jews?" I replied: "Nothing." Sidney then put in quite a large gift.

My next official Inter-Parliamentary Union visit was to Peru in 1959. The Treasury would only allow us first class travel outside the U.S.A. to save dollars, which meant that on the return journey, after our delegation were shown off with great pomp and publicity at Lima, we had, much to the amusement of the other passengers, to remove ourselves into Economy Class seats when we went over U.S.A. territory. We were the first I.P.U. delegation to visit Peru ever from the U.K. and I must say our reception was superb. But I did not come away with the impression that Peru is very democratic or so very keen on practising our parliamentary system.

It is, however, the only South American country I found where the upper classes actually take part in the Government of the country—elsewhere they are just rich and develop lands, mines etc. for themselves. The French seem far ahead of us in their efforts to start up industries and take on long-term development plans. When we were in South America it was very much at the time of France's troubles in North Africa and there was quite a rush of North African French refugees to take on work in Latin America. I came back via Bolivia and right across Brazil and was asked to speak on the Floor of the Chamber at Rio—this was before the new capital, Brazilia, was built—but it was not a very formal affair, since three or four other people seemed to be trying to speak at the same time. When, however, we moved to the Senate, I was taken into the President's Room with quite a few

Senators and we all drank to the health of Princess Margaret. The fact that she had just decided not to marry Group Captain Townsend had so captured the imagination of the Brazilians that my Senator friends would speak of nothing else.

I ask myself sometimes what good the I.P.U. really does? I believe that it does good when it brings people from other countries to our shores.

We have a parliamentary tradition to show and I have helped time and time again to take foreign delegates all over England, Scotland, Wales and Northern Ireland and I know that they have been greatly impressed. But the countries to which we go, as fellow Members—how many of them have really parliamentary Governments or care a bit about Parliaments in the sense that we do? We usually cannot speak their languages and we do not take anything like enough care as to who we send out. Some of our Members, both Socialists and Conservatives, are apt to tell our hosts just where they are wrong, which offends them, and too many of our Members who go out, just go out for the fun of a good trip. How many of the delegates we send ever do anything more about the countries we have visited when they return, beyond attending a party or two at their Embassies? Again, what about the selection of delegates? Arthur Lewis has often raised the question of why some people over the years never get asked to go at all and yet others always seem to be getting these free rides. I in no way criticise the annual or semi-annual conferences (as distinct from the exchange visits), which take place internationally. The discussions there are more serious and detailed— but even then it always seems to be the same people who go out every year.

There is yet another organisation, the Commonwealth Parliamentary Association. This purports to do for the Commonwealth what the Inter-Parliamentary Union does for other countries. I believe here far more is done to help our fellow Members from overseas and I know how deeply its work is appreciated. But many C.P.A. representatives have said: "Yes, we do enjoy going to all the different parts of the Commonwealth and particularly we like meeting new faces, but we do get terribly tired of always seeing the same people coming out as the U.K. Delegation." In the twenty-five years I was a member of the C.P.A. I was only once asked to go on a delegation and it impressed me more than I can say—this was to the then British Guiana, now Guyana. We were a delegation of four just before Independence in 1967 and were led by Bill Whitlock. No one could have done it better—someone must have let him down in Anguilla. I found him an ideal leader and we certainly had difficulties and headaches over Dr. Jagan and his imprisoned supporters. Whitlock steered carefully, and successfully, through every problem. I went out on my own and came back on my own so that I was able to do a little more C.P.A. work in Bermuda, Antigua, Barbados, Trinidad, Grenada, Jamaica and the Bahamas. It was just as these countries were achieving Independence and it was at the moment that free entry to this country was being stopped and our racial problems were coming to a head.

CHAPTER XI

AT HOME FOR BRIGHTON

STILL IN 1945, I was dining one night with Lord and Lady Kemsley at that superb house of theirs, Chandos House. After dinner I found myself talking to Doreen Lady Brabourne; she was cross-questioning me about the Royal Pavilion in Brighton. I told her that, thanks to Queen Mary and the local Curator before the war, Mr. Roberts, it had been saved, but only just saved and there was talk at that moment of pulling it down. It seemed to be falling to pieces and there was no future for it, the local Council insisted. I disagreed as it was something unique. She then unfolded to me a plan that she and Lady Birley, the wife of Sir Oswald Birley the painter, had in mind.

They wanted to hire it for a Regency period Exhibition to raise funds for Mrs. Winston Churchill's favourite charity, the Young Women's Christian Association. I was enthusiastic about the idea, even if I thought the charity a little inappropriate for George IV's favourite palace of fun. But it was undeniable that the country was now just itching for a little fun and colour after the war. Even Ernest Bevin had told us that he wanted the workers of England to get a few weeks relaxation at the seaside to recover from the war strain. It was pretty well all that could be offered them, there was little food to spare and few coupons for clothes. We realised that the lack of materials and coupons might well upset or hinder plans for a big exhibition, but it was worth trying—especially thought I, as it might help my new Regency Society which the Duke of Wellington had just launched for me.

Lord Kemsley lent Lady Brabourne his car to go home and she said that she would drop me at Victoria. She promised that she would straight away get hold of Lady Birley who lived at Alfriston, just outside Brighton, and she would 'phone me next morning. Sure enough, next day—a Saturday—arrived Lady Birley accompanied by Victor Warrender (now Lord Bruntisfield), at my Regency house in Royal Crescent, Brighton. And after an hour's talk we had laid the foundations of our plan.

To cut a long story short, these two ladies worked like slaves. They rushed around to obtain guarantees. I remember Lord Southwood, the head of Odhams Press, guaranteed £1,000 and we soon had all the money we required. We went to see Mr. Clifford Musgrave, the new Curator of the Pavilion, and my staunchest supporter behind the scenes in starting the Regency Society. He soon was enthusiastic and persuaded the Council (who thought that we were quite mad) to let us have the Pavilion for several weeks. Experts in the decoration of the period (it was just beginning to become fashionable again) were quickly roped in, and a Committee was formed. On this were people like The Hon. James Smith (Director of W. H. Smith & Sons), Mrs. Johnnie Dewar (who lent her suite in Claridges for London Committees), Ernest Whinney of Whinney Smith & Whinney—my old firm—who did the accounts, and Lord Bessborough who became our President. I became the Chairman and also the link with local bodies and groups. It became for a bit quite a full-time job and Ian Tucker was taken on as our Secretary. He had a gorgeous sense of humour, never flapped and flattered everybody up to the hilt so that they thought it was they who were doing all the work. His assistant afterwards married Toby Low, M.P. for the rival resort of Blackpool and later Lord Aldington. Let us hope it gave her experience for her next job as wife of a seaside resort M.P. But we did not stop at just redecorating and redoing the Pavilion; we turned it into a fortnight of gala for Brighton—the forerunner of the present Festival.

There were not very many local people in prominent official positions who knew much about Regency—but we roped them in for other things and they were both enthusiastic and wonderful. Mr. and Mrs. Charles Wakeling were outstanding in their efforts.

They helped us with the Stadium; they, and Major Carlo Campbell, put on a tremendous Boxing Display at the Dome. The
Directors of the Theatre Royal where the Regent used to watch
performances regularly, went out of their way to get plays suitable and there were poetry readings. Lastly, we had a Regency
Cricket Match, authentic in every way and in period dress, and
the Brazilian Ambassador bowled the first ball in a howling gale
on the Lawns just off the sea. To crown everything, the present
Queen Mother—then the Queen—came down with Queen Mary
and spent the whole afternoon touring the Exhibition. They later
went on to tea with the grand old lady of Brighton and Hove,
Mrs. Wodehouse, who had already given a Regency Room to the
Hove Museum and whose little grandson, Lord Dufferin, then
aged eight, received the two Queens with full solemnity. It is
interesting to reflect on the times, that Queen Mary wrote to Mrs.
Wodehouse telling her not to worry about a big tea as she would
bring her own rations—to which Mrs. Wodehouse replied begging her not to worry as she was able to procure Queen Mary's
favourite sardine sandwiches!

The whole fortnight ended with a tremendous Fancy Dress
Ball of the period. It was not easy to get the clothes, but we did
somehow and Mrs. Shirley Woolmer ably assisted by Sir Michael
Duff, made a superb Britannia holding court. There was only one
small incident but it was a sign of what would come over the
years. The Mayor complained that he was being charged for his
and the Mayoress's tickets and, as the Pavilion was by custom the
Mayor's property, he expected to eat and dance free. As it was
all for charity Lady Birley would not give way, but we did get,
and lend free, two beautiful period costumes for the Mayor and
Mayoress.

This Festival was read about the world over and the town
obtained superb publicity at no cost to themselves. It opened the
Council's eyes to the fact that it might not be wise to pull down
the Pavilion. Still the powers that be were jealous and did little
to thank either Lady Birley or Lady Brabourne. These, however,
did not care. They had done a superb job; they were able to
pay back all the guarantees and give a good sum to their charity.
In addition they made £8,000 profit which they put aside for

further exhibitions and were able to buy for the Pavilion the huge circular Regency carpet which had previously been at the Czar's Palace at Tzarkoe-zelo in Russia; it is now a proud possession of the town. In two years after this, 1947 and 1949, our same organisation put on the Exhibitions which were equally successful, but the idea we were pressing of making a Festival rather like in Edinburgh was frowned on by the Town. The reason being, I suppose, that private enterprise was running it and not the Council: and so we eventually packed up. Now in the last three years we see a new attempt at a Brighton Festival, which is certainly costing the ratepayers a lot of money and I would not personally swear that it is giving them all the fun our one did—but, at least, the Corporation has taken over the sweat and worry of running an annual exhibition in the Pavilion and for that I believe, we have the perseverance of Mr. Clifford Musgrave to thank.

It was obvious after the war that Brighton had to be completely overhauled and prepared for post-war tastes and in this I tried to take my part. First of all, we started the Regency Society to save Brunswick Square and other central squares, streets and houses. We partially succeeded and the Society is now powerful and flourishing.

I was amused at the Regency Exhibition when Queen Mary sent for the Mayor of Hove. She said to him: "I hear that you are thinking of using Brunswick Square as a car park." He gave her, rather nervously, his reasons. Her comment was: "What a pity. Why not leave it as it is?" As he moved back, she turned to me and said: "I hope I did not go too far." It never became a car park.

From Regency we turned to music and the Brighton Philharmonic Society was restarted. I took over the Chairmanship, as I did of the new R.A.F. Association Branch, of the Brighton and Hove Entertainment Managers' Association, of the Polish ex-Servicemen's Club and of various sporting organisations such as the Hove Squash Rackets Club and later on of the Brighton Tigers Ice Hockey Supporters. It seemed to me that, as Brighton was essentially a holiday resort and Mayors only lasted a year each, it was after a major war the M.P.s job to give a lead and attract people to the town. Moreover we were now in Opposition and we had the time to do this work. When we came back into power in 1951 it became less easy and with the exception of one or two real favourites locally, I gradually handed over the chairmanship of organisations, taking on only one new one, the Antique Dealers' Annual Fair.

Sussex was, from 1945 on, the only county of any size in England where all the M.P.s were Conservatives and we agreed amongst ourselves that we should take on such jobs if needed. We decided to meet every few months for a pleasant dinner in the Commons under the leadership of Lord Winterton who was the Member for Horsham and also the Father of the House. He always tried to be as friendly as possible at these dinners and to call us either by our Christian names or nicknames. The Member for Worthing, Brigadier Prior-Palmer, was nicknamed "Minnow", but poor Eddie Winterton always got it wrong and would keep on calling him "Sprat" and wondered why he did not answer! At a particularly jovial dinner we decided that, if Labour remained in power much longer, Sussex would break away like Monaco from France. Brighton would be our capital (some opposition here), the Pavilion would be the Casino (as in Monte Carlo), the Duke of Norfolk in his castle at Arundel would be our Monarch (as Prince Rainier in his Palace at Monte Carlo) and ex-King Farouk of Egypt would be asked to run our Casino and Gracie Fields to let him rent her home at Peacehaven as his abode, since he was already using her Capri hotel as his base. At the end of the evening, led by Winterton, we all ran round the table singing "Sussex by the Sea". There were twelve of us. But in 1964 our group ceased to exist since the solid façade had been breached and Kemp Town had been won by Dennis Hobden for Labour.

We have only once met since then, including Hobden, when I gave a dinner to welcome the appointment for the first time of a Roman Catholic Bishop in Sussex, the new Bishop of Arundel and Brighton, Monsignor Cashman. Very many years ago the late Duke of Norfolk built a superb Parish Church in Arundel, called after St. Philip Neri, the founder of the Oratorians, and at whose school in Birmingham, started by the late Cardinal Newman, the

late Duke and the present Duke had been educated, as well as
Lord Fitzalan, for many years M.P. for Chichester and Conservative Chief Whip. I always felt sure that the late Duke hoped that
one day this Church in Arundel would be a Catholic Bishop's
Cathedral. Well now his wish has been granted and the Bishop,
who once was the Chaplain to the Duke, and later became the
Secretary to the Apostolic Delegate in London (then Archbishop
and later Cardinal Godfrey) and still later Bishop Auxiliary at
Westminster with St. Mary's, Cadogan Street, as his Church, is
probably the most popular Bishop in England. The Bishop told
a nice story about himself, he said: "I am fast beginning to show
all the attributes of the Almighty. I am incomprehensible on Sundays and invisible all the rest of the week."

During my twenty-five years in Brighton I have kept clear, as
far as possible of interfering in municipal problems; and I think
that the twenty-five Mayors plus the four Mayors of Hove with
whom I have worked will agree with this. It has not always been
possible, but usually so. The Council has been officially Conservative, which one would have thought would have made this easier,
but it has not always been practical, since we choose as Conservative candidates many people who, I am sure, have hardly
the faintest idea what to be a Conservative means. It is socially
rather the thing to be a Councillor and many are those who are
more Socialist, or at least Liberal, then they even themselves
realise. Now that we are giving local Councils more and more
authority, this can become very dangerous for us in the years to
come, since few Labour Councillors are anything but Labour
politicians. More is the pity that Independents are nearly all dis-
appearing. Town Clerks have far more power, I find, with a fairly
ignorant Conservative Council than with Labour ones; but
our Town Clerks, especially Mr. Dodd, have done a superb
job.

After the war the then Town Clerk, Mr. Drew, managed
to put the Town back into action so well and so quickly
that I have always thought he should have been given a knighthood. The obtaining of honours for one's constituents is, I feel
a terrible headache. There are so many channels through which
the recommendations must go, that very often the best man does

not get it, because someone somewhere along the line who has the power of veto, just does not like him.

The only spectacular knighthood with which I had anything to do always pleased me, namely that of George Robey. He lived in Rottingdean, Brighton. It seems that if you once refuse an honour, it is very difficult for it to be granted later. After the First World War, George Robey, who greatly amused George V, was rightly offered a knighthood for his wonderful war work but he refused, I believe with the typically generous reason: "No, it is not suitable for a Red Nosed Comedian." The years went on and through the Second War when again, now much older, he still did everything to keep our spirits up; and then one day some Brightonians came to me and said: "As the local M.P. could you not do something about it?" I thought it wisest to go straight to the Monarch's Secretary, Sir Alan Lascelles, and sent him some particulars. He replied that, alas, he could do nothing about it: though if he had the right of recommending, he would do it at once. He suggested that I should approach the Prime Minister, Churchill, and point out to him how appropriate it would be for the Prime Minister of the U.K. to recommend the "Prime Minister of Mirth". He evidently did so and George Robey became one of the most popular Knights—but it was only just in time; he died very soon afterwards with a Memorial Service in St. Paul's Cathedral packed out. Lady Robey has in recent years been one of the most popular of the Presidents of our Conservative Association and of the local Red Cross.

But if I tell of a success I should also tell of a failure. When two-Member seats were abolished in 1950 and Brighton was divided into Kemp Town, Brighton Pavilion and Hove, the whole reorganisation of the new Pavilion constituency was carried out by Alderman Charles Tyson, the hardest working Tory in my area and recognised at Area Conservative Conferences or smaller meetings as quite the most knowledgeable Conservative on Local Government matters. He was one of our very best Mayors and, in the year when Harold Macmillan came first as Prime Minister to the Party Conference in Brighton, a recommendation for a knighthood for him as a Conservative Leader would have to pass through the bottleneck of the local Area. But, since Brighton

9. A Visit to British R.A.F. in Japan (1947).
Stanley Prescott, M.P., the Author, John Paton, M.P. and Harvey Rhodes (later Lord Rhodes, Lord Lieutenant of Lancashire).

10. The Author with the Crown Prince of Japan outside Houses of Parliament on the occasion of the Coronation 1953.

never has given its quota nor anything like its quota to Party Headquarters' funds, his name was never allowed to go forward.

I think that that is hard. People like Charles Tyson who can ill-afford to give money but give endlessly of their time and energy, should not be barred from rewards because other people just won't put their hands in their pockets. I have seen so many workers amongst our poorer supporters giving and giving and giving and working hard as well—but they get no reward, whereas rich people just vote at Election time or give direct to Headquarters' funds where their gifts can be seen. I feel that here is a reform badly needed. The young come in as Y.C.s, but they pass on and get married and seldom come back to do the donkey work. The old are getting too old.

Earlier in this chapter I wrote about the efforts my friends and I made to bring gaiety and culture back to Brighton after the war. In the Commons, the seaside M.P.s tried hard to get the Government to help our towns on the South Coast get rehabilitated. The Treasury sympathised with our arguments that to bring American and other tourists to our areas would bring us dollars—but the Ministries of Fuel and Food hotly resisted. We did not want tourists to eat our rations or to use up our petrol. It seemed a vicious circle but we went on trying. Here are two extracts from what we said—the first is on 22 February 1946:

"For the benefit of the new Government it is only right that for a few moments I should repeat what I have previously said in the last Parliament—a little about the history of the case of the defence areas. After the fall of Dunkirk a stretch of coast line on the South and South-East coasts of England became extremely vulnerable. It looked as though the Germans would invade that part of England at any moment. In consequence of that, the Government, quite rightly, in my opinion, said: 'We must get out the women and children and those who can go so that we can turn this strip of coast line into a defence area,' not for the benefit of Eastbourne, Hastings, Brighton, Clacton and places on the South and South-East

F

coasts, but for the benefit of the whole of England. In consequence, constituencies, towns and villages round the coast were
evacuated to the extent of a 60 to 80 per cent reduction of their
population. In addition to that, there was a ban on visitors.
No visitors were allowed to go into those areas without a special
permit, and the areas in consequence became desolate and
derelict. I wish to emphasise this fact because hon. Members
seem to forget about it. It was not for our own benefit that this
happened; this economic distress and devastation of our areas
occurred for the benefit of the more prosperous areas of England. In those days we had more than our fair share of enemy
action. Dover was shelled, and I believe Eastbourne was the
most consistently bombed town in the whole of England. People
do not realise that, but it is so, and it can be checked up. I see
the Parliamentary Secretary looking surprised, but in fact we
had raid after raid—not a large number of machines, but,
night after night, two, three, four or half a dozen enemy aircraft came over in tip-and-run raids, dropping their bombs
on Eastbourne and flying out to sea again. We had our quota
of damage by the enemy."

This was Charles Taylor speaking, the Chairman of our Coastal
Committee of which I was Secretary. He put the history of our
problem and later I followed it up :

"Since I have been in the House, in the last two years, I
have become more and more depressed, almost to the state of
despair, about the prospect of anything being done for our
areas in any way different from what is being done for the
country as a whole. That is the main burden of my theme. I
feel that we have gone through, as several other hon. Members
have said, a little more than most other parts of the country.
We have not only been bombed—everybody else has been
bombed—but we have been evacuated; we have been banned
for a long period of time; we have seen V.1's going over us
and falling over us. It is true they were meant for London.
While they were coming to London I remember getting a
letter from a constituent who said that, in view of the fact that

the V.1's were definitely meant for London, would I use my influence to see that they were not shot down over Brighton, as they were, unfortunately, occasionally. But we must remember that the people of these coastal areas, which were for long banned areas, were cut off from their relations and got into a 'jittery' state.

"The women of these South coast areas got into such a state of nerves during the war that it has perhaps made them more jumpy with regard to food problems than is the case in many other parts of the country. They are terrified of what is going to happen this summer. They are not ungracious, or unwilling to have people into their areas, but they say that the food situation is bad enough at the moment, and they do not know what is going to happen when the visitors descend upon them. They say that they will not be able to move from their houses and join the shopping queues before everything has been snatched up by the people coming down from London for the day. Can the Parliamentary Secretary give me any encouragement by saying that special arrangements will be made for the regular inhabitants, who own houses in these areas and have lived there throughout the war? I am not happy about the organisation of the Ministry of Food with regard to these areas."

We got promises that things would be looked into, but little more. These debates have gone on for us over the years. The food shortage was over soon after the Conservatives got back to power. But today no Government seems to realise, or will not admit, that tourism is almost our biggest industry and needs help for lodging the tourist.

During these years in Parliament, I fought actively against the nationalising of the railways which not only made so many of my constituents with railway shares poorer, but also, just as important, took away the power of questioning the Minister of Transport at Question Time about railway problems. Now the railways laugh at M.P.s' complaints and we are fobbed off with a meeting of our "Region" once every so often or a buffet lunch and then the season tickets go up.

But nothing specific needing a Bill to be brought in cropped up until near the end of my period of representation and this was the famous issue of the Marina. I took part in the first Bill to give Brighton a Marina which I considered a godsend to Brighton; and Dennis Hobden, the Labour M.P. for Kemp Town in whose actual constituency it will be, worked loyally with me on this. We had against us a very influential Labour group of M.P.s living in his constituency, but sitting for seats as far away as Aberdeen and West Ham. We got the Bill through all right by putting on a private Whip.

After I had retired, a second Bill had to be brought in to make the approaches easier to the Marina. This was lost quite unnecessarily and mainly because nobody bothered to issue a Whip. Dennis Hobden could hardly have been expected to send a Whip to the Conservatives and many of them were absolutely furious that this was not done by one of our own Members.

Gradually, after Harold Macmillan left as Prime Minister, I began to feel that I had had enough of all-night sittings, annual Ward meetings and wine and cheese parties. A younger generation was coming on who quite rightly wanted to make a name for themselves and saw no reason why older people like myself should try to speak as well. It has more and more become the habit to speak in committee meetings upstairs and not bring any differences we might have down on to the Floor of the House. After the shock of Alec Home being forced to go and the changeover of Party Leader, plus the new type of candidate coming into the Commons, I not only decided to go at the coming Election, which I calculated would be about the middle of 1970, but that I should announce it very early. I wanted my Association not only to have plenty of time to choose a new man—or woman— but that we should get a good one before the best had been snapped up.

After twenty-five years I knew my constituents and the type of man or woman that they would want. We had always remained fairly to the right, although we had a tendency to have more left wing members of key committees. That, of course, often happens in a safe seat where the regular right wingers do not bother to work but soon wake up if there is any real trouble. Bit by bit, my younger Members were becoming more and more right wing and as luck would have it we had a right wing Chairman.

I decided to announce my going in 1967. I said, which was true, that by the end of the Parliament (1971) I would be sixty-eight; that I foresaw a fairly tough next Parliament which could bring me up to seventy-two by 1975 and therefore I would not go on after 1971. Very soon, many M.P.s were stopping me in the Lobby and telling me that they thought they would go too. Since then I see that they have nearly all announced their going—but there are still one or two who haven't. They won't have much fun in the next Parliament. Our Leader is not keen on keeping M.P.s on too long. Hints have been given to several. It is in many ways a pity—but if you are not going to be consulted on your past experience—even if you only are a back-bencher—then what attraction is there in staying?

We collected no less than 123 applications for my job. Since then, I see, as it gets nearer the General Election date and it looks as if we might have a sweeping victory, that for later vacancies there are as many as 400 candidates.

My Chairman showed me the applications and I told him what I knew about each one. Of course, some I had never heard of, but at least I knew the ex-M.P.s. Some local people argued why should you choose an ex-M.P.—after all, he has failed somewhere. That I thought the silliest of arguments.

There are many marginal seats in the country with absolutely first-class M.P.s, but when the tide flows against us, of course they get swept away. To my mind it is for them that seats like mine should be available and we got applications from almost an embarrassing number of absolutely first-class ex-M.P.s.

I arranged for my Chairman to meet some of them for drinks or lunch or in the constituency, and he in turn equally met others he liked the sound of, on his own. The inevitable pressures were put on, but I must say neither the Leader, nor Central Office nor the Whip's Office ever mentioned the subject to me, though they knew I was anxious to get at least an experienced and not too young M.P. to take my place.

When it got near to the last twenty I withdrew taking an active interest, though from amongst them I was quite certain which would be the best. Two luckily withdrew and in the end, by an overwhelming majority, Julian Amery was chosen and I think from all I heard afterwards, he got it largely because Mrs. Amery was so superb herself. When she wants to, she can walk away with anything. The only thing Central Office wanted was that we should have the candidate chosen before the Party Conference which took place in Brighton in 1967. Both I and the Treasurer were against this. Alec Home was coming to speak at a luncheon (expensive tickets!) of ours during the Conference and wisely all the candidates intended to be present. Had we chosen one before the Conference there would have been some twenty guests less. When we did finally choose, after the Conference, the *Sunday Times* sent down an ex-M.P. to make a full-scale investigation as to how Julian Amery had got the seat. He found there was nothing to criticise; the constituency, like so many others, had been going steadily more to the right over the months and he was the choice of a big majority.

Once we had chosen someone eighteen years younger than I, a Privy Councillor and an ex-M.P. who had been an M.P. for fifteen years and a Minister, how could I justify staying on and leaving him just kicking his heels when we needed badly someone of his experience in the House? I had done twenty-five years. My Agent, George Wilson, who has been such a wonderful support over the years—twenty years—was also beginning to feel a little weary. Our Association badly needed a bit of a dusting, wonderful though many of its workers are. The only thing naturally that no constituency likes is the expense of a by- election. But I had fought and paid myself for two elections in the old days. We had been in debt, but those days were nearly over, so I felt justified in going at a time when it looked as if Amery would have nearly two years to find his feet in a new House of Commons.

At the Annual General Meeting in early March 1969 I made my farewell speech and Julian was adopted. Six of us, the Amerys, Lord Lumley (now Lord Scarbrough) who was looking after his transport for the election and the Romillys who were also helping, then motored over to Birch Grove, Mrs. Amery's father's house, Harold Macmillan's, where we had supper and stayed the night. Just as we were going to bed Harold Macmillan turned to me and said : "This must be a very sad day for you." In a sense it was, but it gave me a freedom that I have been looking forward to for so long.

CHAPTER XII

THE CHANNEL TUNNEL

B ETWEEN THE wars there was a very flourishing Channel Tunnel Committee at Westminster, and when Ramsay MacDonald was Prime Minister it nearly won the day, losing by only seven votes in a Division proposing that the Tunnel be started. Amongst those who voted for it were Winston Churchill and Leslie Hore-Belisha. In France it also had a great following led by Marshal Foch. Its greatest enemies were Sir Edward Spears, Lord Montgomery and Lord Hankey, the latter principally because he was afraid that it would put small harbours and small boats out of action and make us unable to defend ourselves if anything were to happen to the Tunnel. During the last war Churchill often thought of it, but the length of time to build it made it in wartime an impracticable project.

After the war, the old Channel Tunnel Company, or, to be more precise, its chief private shareholder, Leo d'Erlanger, kept the idea alive, paid for a very small secretariat and encouraged a Committee in Parliament by paying for more or less annual excursions to Paris to meet our opposite numbers in the French Chamber, at one time led by the French Premier Laniel and later by the present one, M. Chaban-Delmas from Bordeaux. A well-known Labour M.P., Mr. Thurtle, was for years our Chairman, and on his retirement Christopher Shawcross, Sir Hartley's brother, took over. When he gave up being an M.P. he was made a director of the Tunnel Company and Malcolm Bullock took over the Chairmanship of the Tunnel venture. I think that he believed in its possibility, but his wife's family, the Derbys, rather laughed it to scorn, especially Oliver Stanley, and so he never pushed it very hard. When Malcolm left the House I was elected

Chairman in 1955 and I remained so until I retired in 1969 from the Commons.

I had thought at one moment of writing a book about the Tunnel venture and was slowly gathering material in Paris, when one day I got a telephone message asking me to go and see Monsieur Georges-Picot, who was then head of the Suez Canal Company. He pointed out that in less than ten years the lease of the Canal would come to an end and it seemed a great pity that a group of such eminent French and Englishmen as the Directors should just fade out when they had so much money in hand and there were so many possible Anglo-French projects that could be developed—as, for instance, the Channel Tunnel. I came away rather excited. It might then be likely to develop after all. But we did not have to wait ten years. The very next year the Suez trouble started and Georges-Picot suddenly appeared at the House of Commons. He told me that his engineers and experts had to leave and that he must pay them for at least two years. How to use them? We must start a study once again of the Tunnel's possibilities.

About the same time as this, people were beginning to talk more and more of the Common Market. If this were to develop and we were not to be let into it, then to sell our goods in the Common Market area we must be able to sell them much more cheaply. The cost of loading and unloading at our ports and the Continental ports was much more fantastic than anyone realised and a Channel Tunnel with trains or trucks running right through from the North of England to the West of Germany and Italy would give us a tremendous help. Also, around this time the possibilities of getting foreign money to this country for tourism were beginning to be realised much more seriously. People would come, it was argued, much more willingly if they did not have to face a rough Channel crossing. Soon our Committee grew and grew. Leo d'Erlanger and Georges-Picot would, I think, have gladly carried tests through themselves, but there was the French Tunnel Committee to be reckoned with—with large Rothschild interests and the shares held by the French nationalised railways— there were our own newly nationalised railways carrying in the name of the Southern Railway a large block of our own Channel

Tunnel Company shares. Add to this, the new tendency in England to nationalise everything and the equally strong determination by a group of Americans not to be left out, this pushed everyone towards forming an international syndicate. On this were Lord Harcourt of Morgan Grenfells, Sir Ivor Kirkpatrick, until recently Under-Secretary of State for Foreign Affairs, Monsieur Armand, the brilliant French railway engineer and finally Monsieur Massigli, until recently French Ambassador in London, all with Mr. Al Davis to represent the American interests and with Leo d'Erlanger quietly guiding everything.

We were very hopeful of immediate success—but already other interests were at work. The French Routier organisation responsible for the Mont Blanc road tunnel, were determined that there should be a road tunnel and if that were not possible then a Channel Bridge and Monsieur Badevant had his own plans for a road and rail tunnel.

General De Gaulle was in favour of the Tunnel. (*"Madame, moi, je suis Tunalist,"* he told Lady Dixon, our Ambassador's wife at dinner). But Harold Macmillan told De Gaulle when he was about to raise the subject on another occasion: "I'm afraid I know very little about it, except that Lady Dorothy hates the crossing, she always feels sick."

De Gaulle was offended. Marples, then Minister of Transport, said he would not risk Government money in it and that as far as he could see the French said that they were for it *"en principe"*, but they never got down to details. We, of course, had debates on the subject in the House and in one I was continually being called to order by the Speaker because I explained how we could easily have a tunnel from Northern Ireland to Wigtownshire or, failing that, across the Irish Sea to Wales; then another from near Gibraltar to Tangiers so that in fact we could one day travel from Cape Town to Dublin without changing trains. I was about to continue and tell of what was happening to link Hokkaido in the North of Japan with the mainland, but this was too much for the Speaker. When eventually we got back to our main Tunnel, we did get it out of the Minister (Hugh Molson) that there was nothing now to stop a tunnel except finance and that there were no longer any strategic objections. He told Lance Mallalieu and myself how worried he was about us both, because whenever we saw a tunnel we both seemed to want to burrow down and he hoped that we would not get myxomatosis. He announced that an expensive study would be immediately started and the latest machinery, as used by the biggest oil companies in the Gulf of Mexico and elsewhere would be put into use. It would take time.

I spoke rather sadly about this to Gladwyn Jebb, then Ambassador in Paris and later to become Lord Gladwyn. He commented that he could not see the point in this fresh study; surely we knew it was feasible and needed and we had enough information already. Imagine my surprise some time later when he had retired from the Diplomatic Service, that I should find him organising a Group against our tunnel and to build instead a bridge; and then again, on a visit to Paris, the new British Ambassador, Sir Pierson Dixon, told me that he wanted us to get into the Common Market first and then have the Tunnel as a sort of final achievement.

As long as it was suggested that Government money might be involved there was always a danger of it becoming a political issue with some M.P.s pressing for a preference for hospitals and for better roads—but since it became clear that, given a reasonable return, only private international money would be used and then only 25 per cent British money and that if that extra 75 per cent of foreign money was not used it would not come to this country anyway, those complaints seemed to have died down; but others keep arising.

Bill Deedes, M.P. for Ashford, an area likely to be affected, seems to lead this opposition and poor Albert Costain, my Vice-Chairman, is much worried since in his Division, Folkestone and Hythe, there is now increasing opposition due to the likelihood of more and more people and factories coming to the area. An awful lot of rebuilding has for ages been needed by our harbours and also the French ones. These have been postponed because of their not being necessary if there is a Tunnel. But when will it come? I always said "by 1967", but we are now in 1970 and I fear at least two years off a real beginning. Every change of Government, indeed of Minister of Transport, in both this country and France seems to put things off a little longer. After I had been Chairman of the Parliamentary Committee for years, Labour came back to power and so my main Labour supporter, Lance Mallalieu, joined me as Co-Chairman and now has taken over more or less completely, with Commander Powell as Secretary.

Marples was at first against it; Reggie Maudling just doesn't think that it will ever happen; Barbara Castle seemed at one time keen, and Marsh, a most successful Minister of Transport, wrote me a charming letter when I retired; but Leo d'Erlanger did the nicest thing of all, he gave me a superb dinner with his chef and cellar both vying to make everyone cheerful.

I wonder, however, as we all get older, whether d'Erlanger or Commander Powell who has slaved for this so hard behind the scenes, and Don Hunt, the Tunnel Company's P.R. Officer, will ever see it in action. Each year increases the cost; it must take five or six years from its commencement and yet I believe it is the most certain thing to bring Europe and Britain together. It is to date one of my biggest disappointments. All M.P.s can do is to push and nag. This we did at the start, enough I believe to make the Press take note and to make the City and international finance take it seriously. The City then went into a huddle with the different Governments, after which everything has been handed over to the technicians. What happens next is anybody's guess. In the outside world, at least in England, there is a most enthusiastic body, the Channel Tunnel Association, who were good enough to make me their President. They, I believe, have not lost faith, nor should anyone, since so much money has been spent on the idea and the results have been so encouraging. I feel it must work out; but when?

General De Gaulle was keen on it as long as we kept it in international private financial hands. When Monsieur Pompidou and Monsieur Couve de Murville came over in 1968, we gave them a *vin d'Honneur* on the Terrace of the Commons. Lance Mallalieu, my co-Chairman, came up to Monsieur Pompidou and said cheerfully: "Oh! *Monsieur le Premier Ministre*, you look so well, how can you with all your cares?"—we had just been discussing the certitude of the Tunnel—he smiled and replied:

"Ah, you see I am not like your Prime Minister—I have someone behind me—I do not have to worry so much." In those days he was, of course, able to refer to De Gaulle.

The next public step must be the bringing in of Bills both in Paris and at Westminster. If Mr. Peter Walker is Minister of Transport I shall not be too optimistic and when I last saw Monsieur Georges-Picot he sounded very pessimistic.

CHAPTER XIII

CATHOLICS AND WESTMINSTER

I GOT MY greatest insight into the strength of faith amongst
the average Catholic worker in the United Kingdom when
someone in 1932, I do not know who, had a brilliant idea
for 1933, which was the year when the then Pope, Pius XI, had
decreed that there should be a Holy Year to commemorate the
nineteen hundredth anniversary of the death of Our Lord.

The idea was that, as so many well-to-do Catholics could not
get away from the United Kingdom and Ireland in that year
to get to Rome, instead they should give a donation towards
enabling as many of our unemployed, sitting at home depressed
and doing nothing, to be taken to Rome for the celebrations. The
Catholic paper *The Universe* took up the idea, funds were raised
and over 400 unemployed were enabled to go. But how to choose
them? The charming job was left to me and I had also to organise
getting the pilgrims from Great Britain, Wales and all Ireland
to Rome via London. A lot of the Irish were very frightened to
go through London, or even England. They did not breathe freely
until they reached France. We decided to let Parish priests choose
their men and a certain percentage were to represent Catholic
organisations.

The spiritual leader was Father Martindale, the famous Jesuit,
and with me came also Sir Martin Melvin, a wealthy Birmingham
Catholic and as his chaplain a Birmingham Monsignor whom I
then met for the first time—Monsignor Griffin, later to be
Cardinal Griffin, Archbishop of Westminster. Tom Driberg came
to cover the Press (except for *The Times* whose special
Correspondent I became). Tom did not take to Sir Martin, and
afterwards referred to him in the *Daily Express* as "a gentleman

who gives himself in *Who's Who* the proud title of 'owner of *The Universe*.' " I don't think that I made many enemies from the Parish Priests whose candidates I had to turn down, and we really were an impressive body.

The Fascist Government were very good to us in that they waived all passport and visa necessities, taking just one sheet of paper with everyone's signature on it—including Monsignor Griffin and Hugh Delargy's brother, now alas, dead. Cooks provided the transport and food, but we had to sit up night and day.

Not unnaturally, from wherever our unemployed came, the local good nuns and organisations made quite sure that their men had new clothes and would look their best for the Pope. Result: when we got to Rome the photographers thought, "Good God, the unemployed in Britain don't look too poor" and one paper had over a photograph the caption: "The *'Dolce fa Niente'* British Unemployed." The Fascists insisted on only one thing and I was anxious that it should happen—we were taken to see the Dopolavora Sportsfields and all that they were doing for their workers. At our head was Sir Martin Melvin, a millionaire I believe; and when I presented him to the Minister he was immediately given a tremendous speech on Italy's sympathy that he and his friends were out of work, and a hope expressed that he would soon find a job.

Next day we were lined up in the Vatican to see the Pope. He first received me very kindly in private audience and our etiquette-sticklers were horrified that on entering his library I only went down on my knees twice and not the regulation three times! How things have changed now! He said how glad he was that we had gone to see the Catacombs first, as it was out of that setting and humble beginning that the splendour of Rome had gradually developed. He used this later as his theme for his speech to the 400. They were all grouped as from different areas or in organisations. Sir Martin insisted on walking with the Pope and telling him in rather bad French who they all were. He got a bit muddled and when we came to the group of deaf and dumb unemployed who were standing next to the "Back to the Land Movement" he told the Pope that they represented the *"Retour-*

ner à la terre" movement. This meant nothing to the Pope who, of course, had equally no results from the deaf and dumb. Many organisations had sent their banners or other insignia to be specially blessed and the Pope's staff, thinking that these were presents for the Pope, just took them away, to the horror of the poor people responsible for bringing them back to Britain. It was an unforgettable occasion and showed the faith and the courage of these people. I often wonder what happened to them in later years. In four years it will be forty years since they went out. Could not *The Universe* try to trace some of them?

In other chapters I have told of Catholic links with Ireland and of the Catholic Emigration Society which I once ran. It is my considered opinion that the influence of Catholicism on British politics is very greatly exaggerated today and the belief that it does exist somehow, is responsible for there being in the Commons today far fewer Catholic M.P.s than there should be, given the number of Catholic voters.

That of course was not so up to the nineteen-twenties. Until then, there were over a hundred Catholic M.P.s at Westminster coming from Irish constituencies, and the Bishops, and even the Vatican, were fully aware of that influence to protect Catholic ideals as regards education, divorce, abortion and the like. But once Ireland broke away those M.P.s ceased to exist and there were only left the twelve Northern Ireland M.P.s from extreme Protestant constituencies. This, over the next twenty-five years, considerably affected thought in Malta, Gibraltar and other Catholic areas of the Empire, especially as regards integration since they, too, do not like abortion or divorce.

We perhaps even forget that the first woman elected to Parliament was not the late Lady Astor, but an Irish Sinn Fein rebel, Countess Markievitch, the wife of a Pole but actually an Irish Protestant lady (Miss Gore-Booth and the aunt of Lord Gore-Booth, recently head of our Foreign Office); she refused to take her seat because she would not take the oath and nor would the large number of Catholic Sinn Fein M.P.s.

After those days the influence of Catholicism became less and less in Parliament. The late Cardinal Bourne who died in 1935 said to me once: "I do not wish to see a Catholic Party, or any-

正中書 侍惠 生先林欣

11.   Generalissimo Chiang Kai-shek and Madame Chiang.

12.   Hon. Mabel Strickland speaking against Mr. Mintoff's Party in Malta.

thing like one at Westminster. What I want to see is a larger number of Catholics practising their religion and going into public life and just setting a good example."

All through the nineteen-twenties, except for members of the Duke of Norfolk's family and his relations and Lord Lovat and Francis Blundell, there were no Catholic Conservatives outstanding; and any there were were in the Lords, like Lord Iddesleigh and now Lord Lothian and Lord Mowbray and Stourton. The majority of Catholics were of Irish origin and almost hereditarily anti-Conservative and even these were fast losing their religion because in Dockland and elsewhere the rich settlements insisted on the boys and girls attending their Protestant services. The priests seemed to want more and more money to build new Churches or new schools. That, when I first got into Parliament, was the main problem; the schools question. R. A. Butler with his 1944 Education Act made as good a compromise for us as he could, but the burden on most dioceses has been colossal since then.

Over the years, on our education and any other Catholic U.K. problem, the leading fighters for our cause have been the late Dick Stokes, Lord Longford and Bob Mellish for the Labour Party and for the Conservatives, intellectually, undoubtedly Sir Peter Rawlinson and Hugh Fraser. Since he got back into Parliament in 1955, Wing Commander Grant-Ferris (now Sir Robert) has also done a lot socially to bring the different Christian groups together in Westminster. There he has been helped by a very understanding Protestant, Bill van Straubenzee, who actually lives in Lambeth Palace.

For years I have tried to get our Foreign Secretaries to appoint a Papal Nuncio to the United Kingdom, but they are too frightened of Methodist Protestants. We not only have to make do with an Apostolic Delegate, who is only supposed to be acting as a link between the Catholic Bishops here and the Vatican but, at the other end, we are one of the last four countries with a representative at the Vatican who is not an Ambassador, only a Minister. I had an interesting letter on this subject as far back as 1960 from Sir Charles Petrie, in which he says that he remembers distinctly talking to Sir Austen Chamberlain about having an

L

Inter-Nuncio here and Sir Austen said that he was advised it was not possible because of the Act of Settlement when William III took over from James The Second!

There was a moment, when Selwyn Lloyd was Foreign Minister, when it looked as if something would happen and Archbishop O'Hara, then Apostolic Delegate, came hot-foot to the St. James' Club to discuss it with me; but it came to naught. I wrote to the Foreign Secretary about this in January, 1960: but nothing came of it.

An interesting ceremony took place at Buckingham Palace on 21 May, 1952. Various official bodies who, by custom, are entitled so to do, attended on Her Majesty, our new Queen, to present loyal Addresses—as Cardinal Griffin put it "to assure Her Majesty of our devoted allegiance". The Catholics have had the right to do this for a long time—but there was very nearly drama this time. The Monarch does not recognise the titles of Catholic Bishops and Archbishops. The "Archbishop of Westminster" is not recognised at Court—only as "Archbishop Heenan"—but both our Archbishops and our Bishops will only appear as "Bishop of" or "Archbishop of" so-and-so. But a Cardinal is something quite different. He is recognised as a Prince of the Roman Catholic Church and if he leads a delegation as Cardinal, then all is well. This was the case when the Catholics were led by Cardinal Griffin—our only Cardinal at that time. But Cardinal Griffin had been very ill and no one knew if he would be able to make the grade. Luckily he was. Two M.P.s went; Dick Stokes for the Socialists and myself as senior Conservative Catholic M.P. for the Conservatives. There were representatives of the Peers, the Services and every walk of Catholic life.

One felt so sorry for the young Queen, shy, a little cold, in deepest black. Before the ceremony we had been ushered into the Ballroom and, group by group, we went to rehearse. In one group I noticed Jimmy Edwards looking a little strange and also a little self-conscious. As he came into the middle of the Ballroom he said to me: "You know I feel I'm the only person here who has got to do a twice nightly show at the theatre tonight." Just then the Cardinal came up to me and said: "Surely that was Jimmy Edwards you were talking to? What's he doing here?" I pointed out that he was there in his capacity as Rector of Aberdeen University. "Would you introduce me to him?" said the Cardinal. "I've just been very ill in hospital and he cheered me up so much on the wireless."

As we moved towards the Throne Room, the Cardinal stopped the Protestant Bishop of Birmingham who was coming out with the representatives of the Convocation of Canterbury.

"Oh, Bishop," he said, "I do want you to meet *my* Archbishop of Birmingham. I believe you have never met!"

Early in 1955 I went to Cyprus and Athens and on my way back at the invitation of that prominent Catholic lady in Malta, Miss Mabel Strickland, I turned back from Rome and went on to stay with her at her lovely Malta villa. She was getting more and more worried about developments in Malta, especially over Mr. Mintoff's theories concerning integration with the United Kingdom. If what he planned took place, then she felt that the position of the Catholic Church in Malta would be in some danger. The Archbishop felt the same and so, of course, did Mr. Mintoff's opponent, Dr. George Borg-Olivier, the leader of the Nationalists. Miss Strickland wanted to see if I could help in any way. At that moment Churchill retired and Anthony Eden took over the Premiership. It seemed inevitable that there would be a General Election. Once that was over, I promised to help the Nationalists and Miss Strickland in any way I could. We found a very good public relations officer in Colonel Hubert Williams, who had in years gone by worked closely with Sir Walter Monckton in trying to help the Indian Princes and especially the Nizam of Hyderabad.

I undertook to represent the Malta Nationalists at Westminster and as time went on I came to admire and like Dr. Borg-Olivier more and more. Here was a man with a political party in Opposition with no funds, not a very good English speaker and definitely not popular at the Colonial Office. With his quiet dogged determination he fought against Alan Lennox-Boyd, the Colonial Secretary, who was acting on behalf of the new Prime Minister, Eden, who was pro-integration: and also against the whole British Labour Party. Mintoff as Prime Minister came to London as often as he wanted to and was advised by the famous Dr.

Balogh. Miss Strickland, who had her own newspaper to help her, came over, but poor Borg-Olivier could never afford to travel, except when there was a Round Table Conference and the U.K. paid. Miss Strickland did what she could to help him, but she had her own political party. He had a powerful friend in the Archbishop and a great ally in a very brilliant secretary of his Nationalist Party, Victor Ragonesi. For some time I represented the Nationalists in London and even held Press Conferences for them since they could not afford to come over. I went to Malta and Miss Strickland put me up. I also went to Rome and I saw Cardinal Tardini.

But, bit by bit, I began to realise that the Catholic Church was becoming too involved in the dispute, especially should Mintoff and Eden reach agreement. They nearly did, but Mintoff in the end over-played his hand. Even Lennox-Boyd lost patience with him. Finally Borg-Olivier won an election, largely with the help of the Church and the Archbishop (who, it should be remembered, had once himself been a Labour member of the Maltese Parliament), and we turned to his alternative to integration— Independence within the Commonwealth.

Miss Strickland here parted company with Borg-Olivier. From then on I shall never forget the negotiations and indeed the humiliations that the poor Prime Minister of Malta had to go through at the hands of the Colonial Office and, I'm afraid, of our own Conservative Colonial Secretaries. Once the Prime Minister was kept hanging around at the Savoy for over five weeks without any proper meetings with the Colonial Secretary, who was too busy giving other Colonies away. But he never gave in.

By now he had got the strong support of the new Governor, Sir Maurice Dorman. I have still got a letter from the Governor in which he vividly describes Borg-Olivier's problems when coming to London. "Like," as he put it, "a man being let loose in a main street trying to get what he needed for his family only to find that about nine different shops would have to be visited and most of them telling him that it was the other shops who supplied what he wanted."

In trying to obtain his needs he had to see the Colonial Office, the Treasury, the Admiralty, the Defence Ministry, the Air Ministry, the Board of Trade and so on. It was enough to drive anyone mad. There were moments when everything looked black and everyone was depressed in the Savoy suite—especially with Mintoff and the dock workers waiting at Valetta.

But in the end he won through. On the last night in the Commons I had been begged by the Whips not to speak as it would certainly irritate the sections of the Opposition who were hostile to the Church's position in Malta and at all costs Sandys wanted the Bill rushed through that night, so I sat at the back talking to Victor Ragonesi. I had spoken in most of the previous debates and I have some charming letters of congratulation from Dr. Borg-Olivier which I shall always treasure. Victor said to me (it was already 2 a.m.): "Let's go out and get some food." To which I replied : "There is nowhere now where you will get any." "Don't be silly," said Ragonesi. "You don't think that after weeks of being made, with George, to sit at the Colonial Office arguing with Duncan Sandys and only getting, now and then, a sandwich, we haven't found places where we can get food to eat late." They had a hard battle with Duncan Sandys, but at least George Borg-Olivier brought independence to Malta.

Next came the problem of how to attract money and people, how to replace the Forces which were being withdrawn, and generally how to make a new but small nation. That too the Nationalists have achieved and today everyone sings the praises of Malta and most people hope to see the Prime Minister returned once again. The festivities for Independence, graced by the Duke of Edinburgh, were superbly organised and Dr. Borg-Olivier invited me out as his personal guest.

One day I will write a separate book on all that happened over those few years in Malta and I have kept quite enough papers to do so, but too many people are alive who could be offended. It must wait some years. Suffice it for this, that I helped a little to bring about the safety of the Catholic Church in Malta today and the healthy economic situation. Much has still to be agreed with the U.K., but the main points have been gained. Our Treasury seems now the main stumbling block.

The only Catholic enclave now left in our Commonwealth in

danger, is Gibraltar. Spain has her eye on the Fortress. Spain
may one day become as anti-Catholic as she was during the Civil
War before Franco saved her. Gibraltar's great fear is that she
might be sacrificed by a United Kingdom thinking only of trade.
It is a problem in which I have, during the last few years, taken
an active part, even though I am deeply fond of Spain. The
Gibraltarians are not Spaniards and never have been. Many has
been the time when people have said that Gibraltar was no longer
of any use to us. How wrong they have been proved to be! Even
now the latest submarine inventions make the Rock of the greatest
use to us. Gibraltar can be like Hong Kong. We must not give
the people up and somehow I feel that we will not; but the
Mediterranean is now becoming a great Russian centre of influence, and we must guard its entrance.

The British Government today, to pacify the Board of Trade,
might gladly hand over Gibraltar. But it is the Gibraltarians
themselves who will not be handed over, as our own "Gibraltar
Lobby" point out. We are always hearing about our rights and
duties under the Treaty of Utrecht of 1713, but surely, when
later in the eighteenth century Spain attacked the Rock, that
ipso facto washed out the Treaty of Utrecht?

Much more important surely is a later treaty, the Treaty of
Versailles in 1783, when Spain once again recognised our complete ownership of the Rock and in return we gave Spain the
Balearic Isles and Florida. Will she be prepared to give us back
the Balearic Isles—and what has she done with Florida? She
sold it to the U.S.A. Will she buy back for us Miami, and let the
Gibraltarians go and live there? In November 1782 Spain let
it be known that if she were offered not only Minorca but also
East and West Florida in exchange for her claim on Gibraltar
she would forego her claim. By the Treaty of 1783 this was done.
By this bargain, very advantageous to Spain, this made us morally,
and ethically, as well as legally, owners of Gibraltar.

The recent changes in the Government of the Rock have
placed in power a very live wire, Major Bob Peliza. His plans for
Gibraltar's future may well revolutionise life there.

*   *   *

My wife was slowly dying from 1952 onwards, of cancer of the brain. She had been ill for some years without our knowing what was the matter. When she died in 1953 I remember not only getting a letter of sympathy from Churchill and the Cabinet but also a touching one from Quintin Hogg starting off : "I cannot go to bed tonight without writing to you about the sad news we all heard today."

After her death the place in Western Ireland—Clonalis—was taken over by her sister, since we had no children. It belonged, and still belongs, to their brother O'Conor Don and has been in their family (with much other areas around it before) since the eighth century. Few families in Europe can boast such an unbroken descent. My brother-in-law, head of the Irish O'Conors, is a Jesuit. My wife and I lived there for ten years.

My own place, Lucan House, outside Dublin, I sold two years after my wife's death to the Italian Legation who had rented it since 1944 when Mrs. Plunket had taken back Luttrelstown, the place next door, where they were living.

I had found myself in 1943 in the unusual position of being an Air Force Officer negotiating with an enemy alien (the Italian Minister) to let him my property in a neutral country. This by 1956 left me without a home and I felt that being so much in England I could not take on an Irish home with no one to look after it. Soon after an old Catholic friend, Sherman Stonor (now Lord Camoys), told me that Mapledurham near his home and on the Thames, was to let and only a Catholic was to live there so that the Chapel could be used. A haunted Elizabethan house, most of which during the Victorian period had been gutted of its original panelling and Victorianised, had been deliberately let go to ruin because, due to a clause in a nineteenth-century Will, none of the last three owners could leave it to their daughters. It must go to rich cousins in Berkshire and their male descendants, called Eyston.

Everything was done to try to save this house with a lovely façade which was being allowed to fall to pieces. I had a Charity Ball there. The charity organisers came and cleaned up large parts of the derelict side of the house. The electricity people had it floodlit for a week. It looked lovely; even the owners came over twice to see it as it might have been. I had the then Minister of Works, Lord John Hope who lived nearby, over one evening and some of the officials at Windsor as well as the Duke of Wellington and Christopher Hussey of *Country Life*. The upshot was the start of a national grant to rescue it.

But somehow the place always brought me bad luck and endless worries, not appreciated by my Brighton constituents who thought I was living too far away anyway. It was burgled, a good friend of mine, an M.P., Richard Fort was killed in a motor crash near my gate; another M.P. friend of mine nearby had a fire and his son was burnt to death. Then came the 1961/62 winter and the pipes burst. After I had been there for four years my friends the landlords sued me for negligence. It cost me nearly £6,000 which presumably went into restoring the place. So much for old friendships and trying to help!

One sometimes wonders how these things can happen. It certainly frustrated me and taught me a very good lesson and so for the last eight years of my parliamentary life I have lived in flats in London or hotels in Brighton. Having Mapledurham, however, was sometimes useful politically. At different times I had both the Archbishop of Malta and Miss Mabel Strickland to stay and to talk on Malta problems; and on another occasion Sir Solomon Hochoy, the then new Governor of Trinidad.

CHAPTER XIV

THE FRUSTRATIONS OF WESTMINSTER

I REMEMBER SO well after the war, lunching alone with Leo Amery in his Eaton Square house. He pointed out that the lack of newsprint was doing the ordinary back-bencher a lot of harm. No longer were back-benchers' speeches printed in detail and often not at all. Before the war one could pick out good arguments from back-benchers' speeches in *The Times* and follow up by seeing how these men developed. Now a few lines at the most and just picking out, perhaps at random, an argument used was as much as *The Times* could give; the *Daily Telegraph* often ended up with the humiliating remark "Amongst those who also spoke were. . . ."

Twenty-five years in Parliament convinces me of the utter frustrations of the present system. I do not say that a few people for one reason or another, luck, intrigue, the right links but at the right moment, or the financial power they possess, will not bring some to success, but I believe that anyone who wants to get something achieved can get it done with less effort and less health strain elsewhere and probably more efficiently. Only Prime Ministers and a few around them—mostly Civil Servants—count.

It has been quite amazing how many people since early 1969 have written either to defend Parliament, or more often to criticise it. Why is this? I fear because of a general malaise and a feeling that our parliamentary system has proved itself hopelessly out-of-date for emerging independent States, and now even for ourselves, and is slowly dragging Britain down.

In all the major things I wanted to do I have been frustrated in the Commons and having recognised, I think in time, that this was going to be so, I set my sights much lower and so had a very good time.

Before the war I had hoped to prepare myself to help in the badly-needed reform of our Colonies, to get to know the people in foreign lands who would be my opposite numbers in the Parliaments of their own countries and to help improve, strengthen and develop our own Empire; and to do so for the good of the world.

My first frustration was not getting into Parliament until far too late; my next that war intervened before I got there. These, of course, were personal frustrations, but after the War I found that people had lost interest in our Empire and felt that we had nothing left to offer; and wanted at all costs to rid themselves of their responsibilities. This was not only the new thinking of Socialists, Radicals and Liberals generally, but also of Conservatives as well. In the case of Conservatives, it was not so much the case of the Back-Benchers but of most of the leaders in Parliament. Churchill was not really a Conservative, R. A. Butler was openly out to get "the floating votes" and he built up a group to make sure of this, which oddly enough included Enoch Powell. He succeeded and brought into the House many people who had even stood as Liberals during or before the War. Then there was a large body of Radicals who saw no future in a centre party and opted to join Labour or the Conservatives.

We were keen enough on being friendly with Europe during the first years after the war, when we were out of power—but when we came back in 1951 Churchill seemed uninterested, and, old though he was, he dominated Parliament and gave us no reason for his change of front. The best of the Empire had already begun to go with India and Pakistan; and thanks to Labour profligacy over the Health Act and the like, there was no money left to think of really improving our Empire or of being much use to the independent Dominions who were beginning to become less and less sympathetic to our nation.

Many of my friends have fought valiantly for what in effect are losing causes, but if the Whips and Civil Servants and Central Office are not behind you, you really haven't a hope in hell of getting anything done.

Before the last war you had at least the chance of support from various organs of the Press—that is, if you had not yet made your name. But since the war, Press coverage of back-bench speakers has sunk to almost nothing. Why? Because Parliament does not matter so much. Broadcasting, television and debates on the screen have taken its place. Any sympathy for whites in Africa; for the Portuguese who, given the amount of their wealth have always, I think been the best colonizers; or the wonderful achievements of Big Business in Hong Kong or Singapore, all this is now anathema to the B.B.C. and receives scant attention from the Conservative Central Office. The B.B.C. only asks to debate on the B.B.C. for the Conservatives those whom the Central Office say are speaking for their Party. They seldom share my opinions.

Neither are there enough reporters in the Press Gallery, and after all they have sometimes to go out and eat—or drink. This was usually when back-benchers were mostly called—between 7 p.m. and 9 p.m.—and, of course, if it was a late night sitting, there was little hope at all of having one's contribution to the Debate reported. Broadcasting has to a certain extent taken the place of the Press, but how many people listen to the inevitably dreary fifteen minutes of "Today in Parliament" which comes on at 10.45 p.m. when most people have heard the news and gone to bed; or at 8.45 a.m. when most men are on the train heading for their offices. The only hope of the back-bencher is that the Whips will hear him—but they mostly want the business quickly finished and would sooner see the back-bencher in the Smoking Room than keeping the House up longer than is necessary.

People often wonder why seemingly qualified M.P.s, if they are on the Government side, are not always willing to take minor office, i.e. be Parliamentary Secretaries. Once you know the ropes you realise why. To begin with, only the Minister is in control and he deals directly with the Civil Servants. Often the Parliamentary Secretaries just sit in large offices and are not consulted at all. If they know anything about the subject they are resented by the senior Civil Servants.

Added to all this is the fact that by being made a Parliamentary Secretary you are cut off from attending Party meetings on indeed any other subject than the Ministry to which you have been appointed. You are, in fact, less well informed on general subjects than the ordinary back-bencher, only being allowed to attend meetings on the one specialised subject. Your frustration is greater than that of the ordinary M.P. and, being a member of the Government, you cannot vote except with the Government.

The lot of Whips is even worse: they must not speak at all. Heath was a Whip for many years—no wonder then that only now is he beginning to be a success as a debater or platform speaker. He is a little like a retarded child but he is fast pulling up.

The days of the Independents also really died when the University seats were abolished; and Labour's determination to have its legislation passed in Committee upstairs has cut the back-bencher off still further. Not everyone realises that, until just after the war, major Bills and in fact most Bills were taken on the Floor of the House—everyone had an opportunity to speak. But when Herbert Morrison became Leader of the House he realised that the programme his Party wished to put through was far too big to find the time. The Committee stage of most Bills therefore was to be taken upstairs with only a small percentage of M.P.s being allowed to take part and vote on each Clause.

The proportion of M.P.s to be chosen were to be in the ratio of the total strength of each Party, which cut our numbers participating down very considerably and, of course, the Whips of each Party were to choose whom they wished to serve on each Committee. This once again put the back-bencher at the mercy of his Whip and his Leader.

Once, in order to fill our quota, the Whips put Sir Gerald Nabarro, at that time as popular nationally as Enoch Powell is becoming now, on either the Scottish or the Welsh Grand Committee—I forget which. His constituency had no interest in any of this Committee's work and it has always been (since 1945) the custom that on the Scottish Grand Committee only Scottish M.P.s spoke. Nabarro insisted on making long but interesting speeches on every possible occasion. The result? The Scottish M.P.s felt that he was using up their precious time and in a fortnight the Whips had pulled him off the Committee.

On the other hand, a Bill vitally concerning my constituency,

Brighton, went into Committee and I had a letter from my Town Clerk asking me to come and meet the Brighton Council to tell me what they would like me to do. When I met them and told them that I was not on the Committee and that I would have to get someone who was not elected for Brighton to represent them, they were highly indignant and realised for the first time how their rights were gradually being frittered away.

Yet another and even more serious back-bencher's right was taken away by Morrison—the right to ask Questions on nationalised industries. During the war and after it, until the railways were nationalised I was always asking Questions on railway problems which greatly worried my Brighton constituents. The Ministries naturally hate these Questions, but it keeps them on their toes. After nationalisation we back-benchers lost that right. We could only write to Civil Servants who either ignored us, or sent us a dusty answer in the post which never saw the light of day elsewhere. It, however, made life much easier for the Civil Servants and only once or twice a year was there a full debate on whatever industry had been nationalised. As Morrison put it: "It would be like an Annual General Meeting of any big industry when the shareholders could question the Board of Directors." So at one fell swoop there disappeared the power of Members of the Commons to keep control over the Railways, the Mines and much else.

To add insult to injury, in cases where the Civil Servants could not foresee developments ahead, they arranged that the Ministers should have the power to bring in an "Order in Council" which would have the effect of an Act of Parliament after thirty days; and the number of these Orders in Council in recent years has been legion. If, before the end of thirty Parliamentary days, nobody has put down a Prayer (nominally to pray the Monarch to withdraw the Order) it becomes *ipso facto* law. At first we, and Labour M.P.s as well, took full advantage of this right to pray and we would sit up all night "praying" against an Order, even though we knew that with the Government's majority there was no hope of getting anything achieved and not even of publicity, since the Press went to print usually before midnight and the B.B.C's report on "Today in Parliament" ended at 10 p.m.

Still, it was a dying kick for Parliamentary independence and, on Labour's side, a brilliant debater and fascinating character from Northern Ireland, Geoffrey Bing, used to arrive with his friends and volumes of Hansard for quotation under his arm, at the appointed time for the Prayer to start—at 10 p.m.—and carry on often until dawn. Sir Beverly Baxter on our side, sighing at the prospect of an all-night sitting, used to dub this group "The Midnight Hags". But eventually the Civil Servants got tired of this; they pressed both Government and Opposition Whips to have a resolution passed that "Prayers" could not go on after 11.30 p.m. As they did not start until 10 p.m. that only left one and a half hours of which the appropriate Minister by custom absorbed fifteen to twenty minutes and that is the position today. Yet another victory for Civil Servants and frustration for M.P.s.

In recent years even the right to ask Questions has been whittled down. Only two Questions a day can now be asked by any one M.P. (That is to say Oral Questions.) It used to be three a day. Until recently there were one or two days a week for Questions to be asked in turn to Dominion Secretaries, Colonial Secretaries and Foreign Secretaries; but as these Ministers gradually crept up from being bottom of the list to be top of the list and then went down again to bottom of the list, it might mean six weeks before you could get your Question answered orally, which can be maddening if something you vitally want brought up in the House takes place say five weeks before the Minister's turn comes to answer again. But, worse still, in the last year, Foreign Office, Dominion Office and Colonial Office have all amalgamated. Does this mean that the Foreign Office, answering for all three, gets some extra days? Oh dear no. You can still only ask two Questions when previously, if you were interested in Colonial as well as Foreign Affairs etc. you got at least six Questions over three different days. Is it any wonder that one feels disheartened?

At least also in the old days you could put your name down for the Adjournment which meant half an hour's debate on your particular problem coming immediately after the finish of the day's official business. But here again things have changed very considerably in recent years. After the war, anyone could apply for the Adjournment but could not get it more than once a month. You had to queue up at one time and it was "first come, first served"; you put your name in a book. Then later on you balloted for it and there were therefore five days a week for Adjournments. But now it has been altered once again. You still ballot for it, but only for Mondays, Wednesdays and Fridays. On Tuesdays and Thursdays your name is still in the Ballot, but the Speaker decides who shall have the Adjournment from those who apply. In effect, this means that in two cases out of every five the Speaker decides what is the most important and topical subject to be discussed. How he does it I do not know, but he cannot be knowledgeable on every subject nor I think is he especially on some sides of Colonial or Foreign Affairs, but what the back-bench M.P. thinks is important has only a much smaller chance of being discussed than before.

It is my considered opinion that over the last twenty-five years the ordinary M.P., whether he is on the Government side or the Opposition side, has gradually lost more and more of his influence on affairs.

Nor do I think that necessarily this power has been transferred to the Government of the day, or to the Leaders of the Opposition, nor to the '22 Committee or other Party Committees. It has been steadily taken over by the Civil Servants. I remember when we got in, in 1951, Sir Philip Warter who had been doing a voluntary job, helping the Board of Trade, telling me how he had seen Civil Servants at work there, knowing that the Tories were likely to get in next and so arranging things that whoever took over would not be able to alter what they wanted done.

I remember when Labour got in before the War, a Colonial Governor assured me that the Colonial Office would never let Labour make a mess of things; but they did, largely because by then the Civil Servants at the Colonial Office were as Socialist as their less-well paid Chiefs and many of them have never visited a Colony.

I remember Alan Lennox-Boyd, when he came to the Ministry of Transport, after Mr. Barnes his Labour predecessor, being horrified at the number of things that were being done without consulting him and how equally horrified were the Civil Servants that he should want to be consulted. "Mr. Barnes always left it to us." Lastly, when Selwyn Lloyd was at the Treasury, he felt that the Treasury Officials were losing control over the expenditure of other Ministries and was quite determined that this should stop; control must be tightened up. Power this time for the Treasury. Today it is as difficult for an M.P. to get things done as the proverbial camel and the eye of a needle.

13.   The Author and Pope John XXIII.

14. The Author and the Rt. Hon. Harold Macmillan, with His Worship Alderman Tyson (Mayor of Brighton). Conservative Party Conference 1961.

CHAPTER XV

HELPING FOREIGN BONDHOLDERS

WHEN I WAS in Tokyo in 1947 MacArthur allowed me to meet the Japanese Ministers and I went one day, alone, to meet the Cabinet. The Minister of Finance lent over and said: "Remember, Mr. Teeling, we always pay our lawful debts and the moment we are allowed to do so, we will repay in full all Japanese bonds." Having known Japan from before the war and realising the Japanese mentality and also knowing the Minister, I felt certain that this was correct. Dalton (who resigned as Chancellor whilst I was on my way back to England) had scoffed at Japan ever paying up. Impatient bondholders in Britain were selling their bonds for literally almost nothing to shrewd City merchants who had heard as I had. There was no time to lose before a Peace Treaty must be pushed through. I started a Japanese Bondholders' Protection Group, held Press Conferences, got funds from the City, went to Paris to get French support as well and finally convinced many people that they should hold on to their shares. Not everyone was on my side. Many other countries were not keen to see Japan pay up in full, lest they should have to do so as well—but we won through with the aid of the Foreign Bondholders' Council, R. A. Butler and Mr. E. J. Speyer who wrote about them regularly in the *Investors' Chronicle*. In Japan also, the Government of Mr. Yoshida was most anxious to help and did so and Mr. Ihara, now I think head of the Bank of Tokyo, came over to the Japanese Embassy especially. He told me that he thought Mr. Speyer had the most brilliant financial brain in the City.

Once the Japanese problem was through and our Parliament had agreed the terms of the Peace Treaty, many other groups came to me and over the next "wasted years" we have gradually got foreign debtors to pay up. It always takes time, but in the end most countries pay. The Anglo-Argentine tramways and the Primitiva Gas Company were our biggest South American worries. Here you had to compete with the Board of Trade, who never wants to alienate a foreigner and will gladly sign with foreigners for big orders and so get paper credit for their balance sheets—but they seem to be quite uninterested as to whether there is a hope of these countries paying back. When I go along and tell them of the plight of elderly people who believed them when before the war, they said the same things about these wonderful foreigners, they just consider me an awful nuisance.

I must say that a more solid City front to insist on repayment of debts before granting credit for new debts, would also help a lot.

One day in 1952, Reggie Maudling and I were coming away from a meeting we had both had at the Foreign Office about the payments to the Debenture holders of the Anglo-Argentine Tramways and the Primitiva Gas Company. He then said : "I am sorry, but I won't be able to come with you any more as tomorrow I am becoming an Under Secretary. I'm rather pleased but my Bank Manager isn't, as I was just beginning to make some money." I have often felt in more recent days that Maudling, not having made his City pile, as have many Ministers before going into politics, has had to watch that side of his career enough to be not unwilling to let Ted Heath be the full-time Leader.

Later, on my own, I remember having a debate on Argentine Tramway debts one evening; nobody in the Commons seemed interested, no matter what they had written about it to their complaining constituents. My audience consisted of the Minister who was replying, the wretched Speaker who had to sit through it and two Whips, one on each side. I did not care. I got my points in and I knew it would be in *Hansard* even if no British paper, except the *Financial Times*, printed it. But two days later I was talking it over with the Foreign Minister and he commented : "We will do what we can, but did you realise that sitting in the Gallery was the Argentine Ambassador? If I send out a message to Buenos Aires that I am being very strongly pressed in the

House of Commons to get something done, he in turn will have sent back a message to his Government saying, 'Don't worry, nobody is interested; there were only four M.P.s present.'" Still we got our settlement when a new Argentine Government came in, wanting more money from Europe.

Oddly enough, the only times one of my debt problems brought reasonable houses in the Commons and in the Lords was when we debated the Baltic Bonds and, equally oddly as I see it, the opponents of the Agreement were unreasonable.

Nobody in their senses can believe that Latvia, Estonia and Lithuania will ever be free again, or at least that the people who originally owned this money will be the people allowed to say: "We are independent." Only history will tell how many people have been taken from these territories and sent towards Siberia, whilst to carry out Russian policy, Tartars and the like have been moved into these East European States.

In the meantime there are in this country numbers of people, almost all coming from the Baltic States, who have lost nearly everything and could be happy again if only part of their losses were repaid to them. This is now being done at the cost of half a million paid to Russia and with Baltic gold. There are, of course, some rather difficult points to explain away, such as why the gold was sold, when there was great pressure on the pound, without authority from Parliament and why no promise was given that, if these countries did get back their freedom, we would repay the money? It would have been a fair risk to take, as the chances are slight, alas, but the main thing to my mind is that the money is being paid out to those who do need it badly and not just held *ad infinitum*.

Other countries, like Hungary, Poland and, I hope, soon Rumania and Bulgaria, are negotiating with us just now, but no one in these areas quite appreciates the typically British attitude that we have a semi-Government financed body called the Council of Foreign Bondholders and yet these countries must negotiate with the British Government as well. It is not within the comprehension of Slav logic, but it is a fact and our Ministers, especially poor George Thomson and Goronwy Roberts, fight on manfully to get something done. I must say that I have found the

Socialist Ministers much more helpful in attempting settlements than the Conservatives have ever been. Is it because the Socialists realised how many small people are hard hit—or is it that the Socialist Government needs the money from abroad more than the Conservatives ever did? That's not for me to say; I'm inclined to think the former.

There remain, however, two outstanding sets of Bonds needing repayment; and by outstanding I mean prominent—the Russian Tzarist Debts and the Chinese Debts. For some people the Russian Tzarist Debts are a little bit of a joke; so were the Baltic Debts ten years ago. When I started to lead deputations to the Foreign Office on these combined debts in the early 'fifties I found that the Foreign Office were not so despondent and every time our Government Leaders went to Russia we were always called in and the whole position reviewed "just in case" as Anthony Nutting once told us "the Russians bring the matter up".

Then, sure enough, one day Russia did say "We will discuss the Baltic Bonds." It was at that time that the Foreign Office promised me that the moment the Baltic Bonds were settled, we would turn our attention to the Tzarist claims. I suggested that it should be the other way round. After all, the Tzarist claims were much longer outstanding; the claimants were older and in many cases poorer and Russia had benefited over the years from the railroads and other developments opening up Russia which these monies had made possible. But it was not to be and the Baltics came first. It took nearly ten years to settle them—but then, sure enough, the Foreign Office kept their word and gave notice to the U.S.S.R. that they wished to have the matter re the Tzarist debts reopened. About four years ago Lord Thomson and a group of our businessmen, who included owners of large blocks of these Russian bonds, went to Moscow. Lord Thomson did not bring the matter up first—it was Mr. Kruschev who did. He said that he would like a large loan from the U.K., but realised that the Tzarist debts must be paid off first. Later I asked Lord Thomson to have a study made of what it all involved. He intended Mr. Rees-Mogg to do this for him, but soon the latter moved to be Editor of *The Times* and we have heard no more about it.

Our Foreign Office, however, quite definitely intends to press the matter and only a few days before I left the House of Commons the Minister of State wrote to me to say that they are pressing on. The French, of course, are equally owed money and are working separately towards obtaining redress. Their Bourse is more optimistic than ours—but, personally, rather than wait several years I would prefer that the British Government took powers and brought in a Bill to take over what monies certain British Banks hold (and use) which came from Russia, just as did the Baltic gold. If Russia will not do anything within a reasonable time, then the Foreign Office have promised me that they will bring in such a Bill. If compound interest is included, those people who still possess the Bonds may get a reasonable sum.

With the Chinese little can be expected in their present mood, but what we have quite forgotten is that those loans which were borrowed from the U.S.A. are being perfectly well serviced by Formosa and that Formosa has written (I have seen a copy of the letter) that they will pay us too as soon as we recognise the Nationalist Government or as soon as they return to the mainland. This too is more of a possibility than many realise.

I do not think it unfair, I have his permission, if I quote here from the Speaker's letter to me of farewell the day I left the House. He says:

"No back-bencher has served more devotedly the cause of international understanding between the free peoples of the world. In addition, nobody has pursued with such tenacity as you have the quest for justice for those who lost possessions in totalitarian countries."

*   *   *

During these twenty-five years I was lucky enough to draw two or three lots to bring in Private Members' Bills. I was unsuccessful in getting one through—namely the authors' rights to have a Royalty percentage on library books. Here, oddly enough, the present Speaker, as a back-bencher, was strongly against me. I had the support behind the scenes of A. P. Herbert, but it was regularly "talked out".

I was much more successful over a Bill to stop dogs worrying sheep—a measure badly needed for the Sussex Downs against trippers' dogs and the number of alsatians which were released by the Forces after the war. This went through in 1953, but the Lord Chancellor, (Kilmuir) commenting on it said: "What a pity it is that dogs cannot read."

A third Bill was the Double Death Duties Bill. This I brought in strongly backed by my old friend Bob Matthew, M.P. for Honiton. We had recently had in Brighton a case where husband and wife died as the result of a car crash and another friend of mine and his wife, travelling for the first time by air, were both killed. Here I had my first, and I think only, personal clash with Enoch Powell. He was then Financial Secretary to the Treasury. He sent for me and said quite bluntly, "You can't bring in this Bill. It is only suitable for inclusion in the Budget, not for a Private Member. You must withdraw it. I would have to answer it in Committee and in the House and I'm not prepared to give the time to it." His whole tone annoyed me and I refused point blank to withdraw it. What would have happened I do not know, because he resigned from the Treasury with Peter Thorneycroft in January 1958 and when it came up for Second Reading his successor agreed to it and promised to put it in the Budget. I insisted on my Second Reading and sure enough we got it in the Budget and indeed a little more, since double death duties were scaled down over the years.

The number of Adjournment debates I obtained over the years need not come into this book. One instance, I brought up on no less than three occasions. It was an appeal for a constituent of mine, Mr. Topham, a Merchant Navy seaman, shot by a policeman in a fight in a bar in Cuba, where thanks to the efforts of Peter Thomas, then Minister of State at the Foreign Office, and the very attractive woman Chargé d'Affaires at the Cuban Embassy, Topham got £8,000 compensation. We had a lunch to celebrate at the House of Commons. Then an attempt to save the Pullman Car Company from being taken over by British Railways; efforts to get the Brighton postal service improved;

efforts to save the Bedford Hotel in Brighton and also to stop Princes' Hotel in Hove being taken over by the Electricity Board, and many other problems, not perhaps of national importance, (though fog-clearing instruments for air fields such as FIDO might be an exception). I was happy to be with Mr. Hector Hughes partially responsible for an announcement in 1959 about the future of the Lane Bequest and the sharing of the pictures between London and Dublin. It was to be for a period of twenty years only. That is ten years ago. What is happening now?

I have often felt deep responsibility for our aged citizens living abroad, many of whom have no relatives in the United Kingdom, or accustomed to a warm climate, could not face English winters, but here again one meets with unnecessary frustrations. The closing of the Nice Consulate General in 1957 was to my mind a particularly silly suggestion at a time when there was a sudden rush for economy. Selwyn Lloyd seemed quite determined to go on with it and our Ambassador in Paris, Lord Gladwyn, evidently O.K.'d the idea.

Briefly, after the war, as Honorary Secretary of the Tourist and Holidays Committee in the Commons, I was asked by the 8,000 to 10,000 British residents on the Riviera to take up their grievances. One of these grievances was the closing down of the British Consulate in Nice, a fine building in a fine setting which had been there for nearly a century; the reason, economy. These 8,000 include Maltese, Gibraltarians, Cypriots, etc. but also many British ex-governesses and poorer people who for climatic and other reasons cannot come back to settle in the U.K. even though the costs of living keeps on going up in France. Add to this the thousands of people coming from the U.K. to the Riviera in the summer who have motor or motorcycle accidents, or who get financially stranded. Then there are the number of small yachts and general shipping, plus their insurance work that has to be done for the Onassis and other interests who prefer to deal with Lloyd's rather than the U.S.A. Nice was an obvious centre, but no, we decided to leave it all to Marseilles which by train involves one night's stop each way, the distance being so far. Selwyn Lloyd was adamant. Nearly every other European country was starting up new Consulates, but no, we must close ours. Even Winston

Churchill, now getting very old, said to me: "It's a sad pity, another link going with the past."

The Consulate, in spite of my debates, was closed—for ever.* Yet in three years time Selwyn Lloyd had to open it up again. There had been no saving, but loss of a lot of prestige, much inconvenience, and the complete loss of a fine building plus the pensioning off of old (thirty years long) staff who had stayed on through the war years, at half the pension an ordinary French worker would have got legally.

The local British had done all they could, especially Robin Ward, Colonel Sawyer and Eric Dunstan; and the poor Consul-General Wolstan Forester had been thrown out against his wishes and before retiring age. That is the sort of frustration I hate.

* *Hansard* [578] Cols 385–6.

CHAPTER XVI

THE FAR EAST AND AFRICA

O NE DAY in 1954, just after returning from Ireland, I had a message from the Chief Whip to come and see him urgently.

I had read in the Irish papers Reuters announcement from Formosa (or Taiwan as it is now called—but I propose to call it Formosa in this book) that I was about to visit the island and that I would be the first British M.P. to do this since the U.K. recognised Red China in 1949. What I did not quite realise was the opposition that I was going to meet. Patrick Buchan-Hepburn, the Chief Whip, told me that Anthony Eden was very worried and did not want me to go. Just at that moment things were very tricky with Red China, especially about trade, and we were also having trouble with the U.S.A. and with Hong Kong. In fact the Foreign Office were in a flap. I said that I could see no harm; Chiang Kai-shek had now been four years in Formosa; the Korean war was over. It was high time someone went to see what was going on and obviously, since we did not now recognise Chiang Kai-shek, it could not be a member of the Government. The Formosan unofficial representative in London had invited me to go out and I knew China well and had many Chinese friends.

The Chief Whip then told me that Eden was bringing the matter up to be discussed by the Cabinet next day. It was; Churchill and Eden were there. I got a personal letter from Eden asking me not to go. There was nothing I could do. What are called "The China Hands" who are the big business interests in the City with vast claims on China were, and I believe are, still convinced that they will make much money again trading with

Red China and they were horrified at the idea of my trip. Had the Formosan authorities not let it be known to Reuters, things might have gone off quite smoothly. I told my Chinese friends that I must wait, but that I was quite determined to go there. Legally no one could stop me.

I waited until after the General Election and until 1956. Then I just quietly flew out, asking no one's permission, to Hong Kong. I arrived there about 7 a.m. I had a further ticket and visa to leave direct for Formosa by 8 a.m. I spent the interval writing to the Governor whom I knew well, apologising for not giving him notice but that, as I was only there for one hour there was no real need, and anyway that I would be back for a day or two in a fortnight's time. By lunchtime I was in Formosa, the first British M.P. to visit our former ally, Chiang Kai-shek.

Then, I gather, the furies were let loose. The Governor wrote me from Hong Kong that he could not put me up on my return, and that he would be away the days I mentioned. International radios interviewed me and the Foreign Office refused to comment on what I said "until they had had the full transcript of my statements". I had a standing ovation in the Chinese Parliament. What lucky M.P.s they were! They sat for constituencies all over China : they could not go back and their constituents could not write to them! The Generalissimo and Madame Chiang received me twice. I met everyone, including our own Consul, who was Acting Consul-General, and who had great sympathy with the Formosan struggle.

After the collapse of the Nationalists in 1949 and 1950, it was an up-hill battle in Formosa, but most of the intellectuals and leading Civil Servants, the best Generals and Air Force Officers (many trained in the U.K.) and most of the diplomats of the former Chinese Government, were there. It was touching to see how fond they were of Britain, with whom, after all, they had no quarrel. I believe that they have never forgotten that I was the first to come from the U.K. Parliament in spite of our Foreign Office's objections. I went again in 1958 and visited Quemoy on the edge of mainland China. I returned again for a Far Eastern Anti-Communist meeting in 1964 when President Nixon, travelling in a private capacity, flew over with me, and I last went in

1967 to celebrate Chiang Kai-shek's eightieth birthday. This was a particular honour as he asked me out as his special guest.

This is one of the most amazing men alive. He is the last survivor of the great war leaders and the way he and his followers have pulled Formosa from a small military Japanese colony, as I knew it in 1935/36, with a population of around four million souls, to its present flourishing condition with nearly thirteen million inhabitants in less than twenty years; with an ever-expanding economy on its own without any longer American assistance; with the best health record in the whole of the Far East; with a vastly increasing Christian Chinese population; and with all the very best of the Imperial Treasures from Pekin enshrined in a superb museum where they can be changed every three months for the next twenty years and still not be a repeat showing, is quite remarkable. All this, plus the immensely important strategic position of the island, for we must not forget that it was from Formosa that the Japanese took off to make their conquests of Malaysia down to the Australian coast—I will write about it in another book some time. There is little doubt but that this is the success story of the post-war world.

It is high time Europe awoke to what has been developing over the years and how we are practically forbidden in the West by Communist underground pressure to know what is really happening and what we are missing. Suffice it that, since I first went to Formosa, we have now had visitors from Parliament, Conservative, Labour and Liberals to the tune of about thirty M.P.s with people as prominent as Geoffrey Rippon, Geoffrey de Freitas, Edward Du Cann, Lady Violet Bonham Carter and Albert Roberts, the Labour Chairman of the Inter-Parliamentary Union, and Tony Lambton, all visiting the island and coming back deeply impressed. We have formed a group in Parliament called The Anglo-Taiwan Group and Sir John Rodgers is its active Chairman, Lord Segal its Treasurer and Patrick Wall its Secretary. Field Marshals have wanted to visit it, but they are never retired and so can only go when the Government permits; and the Foreign Office firmly puts its foot down—the dear Reds who insult and imprison our traders, diplomats and Reuter's representative, must not be antagonised and, of course Field

Marshal Montgomery can gladly go as often as he likes to see Mao Tse Tung. What a mad country we seem to be in!

On my way home from my first visit in 1954 I had a slightly chilly reception in Hong Kong compared to previous visits, but Sir Guy Grantham did give me luncheon and have a long talk about what I had seen and Harold Lee, a loyal friend from the past, put me up as his guest in one of his hotels. I then went on to the Philippines to a warm welcome from my French cousins, Edouard Miailhe who with his wife (née Burke) have interests there. But alas, the day after I arrived the Filipino President was killed in an air crash and the Islands were plunged into gloom.

Sir George Clutton, our Ambassador, thought that, in spite of the mourning, it was a pity to waste a visiting M.P. and arranged for me to call on the Foreign Minister and I did so. Later that day I went to lunch with the Japanese Ambassador who had been in London before and for whom I had a great affection—Mr. Asaki. I told him that my Ambassador was going to represent our Queen at the funeral. This put him ahead of the Japanese Prime Minister and Asaki seemed annoyed. Later in the day I got a frantic message from Clutton that the new Acting-President had told him that he wished me to be at the Palace at 6 p.m. when he was receiving all the visiting Heads of State etc. who were attending the funeral, planned to take place the next day.

I arrived rather nonplussed and was put next in line to the junior Ambassador, the Argentine one. He politely asked me: "When did you present your credentials?" I told him that I had none. But Asaki came up to me looking daggers and said: "You never told me at luncheon that you were here for the funeral too." I tried to explain that I was not, but that I had been roped in after luncheon. I'm sure that he did not believe me. Next time I was in Tokyo he refused to see me, and again when he came to London. I am still very sorry; we worked together to bring about a friendly Peace Treaty and I would have liked to have remained friends.

When we all moved towards the Acting President I saw Clutton make his little speech and as he came back I said: "But what on earth am I to say?" He replied: "Just say you are conveying the sympathy of the Speaker of the House of Commons."

When I reached the Acting President, an old friend of my uncle's who lived in Manila, he said: "I cannot tell you how touched we are that the British Parliament has sent out a representative and that it should be Dr. Burke's nephew."

There was nothing more to be said, but I remembered, rather alarmed, that the funeral was next day and that I was booked to fly to Bangkok next morning. I flew as arranged and I saw my name in the Philippine papers as amongst those present, but as no one knew what I looked like it did not matter. On my return to London I rang up the Philippine Ambassador to apologise. His only comment: "But what does it matter? It will give me greater prestige for having got the Parliament to send someone out."

In Bangkok I stayed with Berkeley Gage, an old friend from my earlier pre-war Chinese days. He had to look after Chinese diplomats and Service representatives in London during the war and now, Ambassador in Bangkok, he was quite determined not to cut them. He managed it superbly; hurt no one's feelings and was the best Ambassador we had there for years.

When I visited Formosa in 1964, I went on to Japan and Korea and in Seoul represented the British at the opening of the Anti-Communist Centre. I was told that I was going to be put immediately behind the President at the Opening. I said to the Doyen of the Diplomatic Corps: "But surely that should be your place—I do apologise." "Ah, no," he replied, "it does not matter. You see we have been told that there is going to be an attempt made on the President's life." I was a bit shaken, since the President was a very small man and I felt more than a little exposed!

After the Korean war the vast majority of the people who are at heart anti-Communist, moved into the South which is far too small to hold them. The North on the other hand has mines, rich agricultural land and a tiny population. Seoul is only thirty miles from the frontier. Today the U.S.A. supports South Korea, but will she continue to do so? Korea and Japan hate each other, the Philippines have their eye on Borneo and Sarawak and in the long run Malaysia. We know all about Vietnam. What future is there for the Far East? And how little we seem to care at Westminster. Even Enoch Powell wishes to be rid of our responsibilities there. But won't this hurt Australia? The only group in Britain interested in the East are the much scoffed-at Moral Rearmament Group. They have a few members in the Commons and just after the war James Stuart asked me to go out and visit them at Caux in Switzerland to show that not only Labour were interested in their work. I am not a member, but they do good and should be encouraged and the death of their leader, Peter Howard, was a real loss to clean living in this part of the world.

*   *   *

Not only is the East a danger spot—so also is Africa. I visited Kenya, Tanzania and Uganda in 1952. Looking back, how right those who had settled there since the beginning of this century were to say: "Rhodesia is all right, she has her own troops, we have not and so we must do what London says and despite the talk in Westminster—what each and every one of whatever party watches is the voting lists at home. If we were left to ourselves we would make a wonderful multi-racial world in East Africa."

We know it is true, but it is only Rhodesia and her problems that have brought this out. Too late for East Africa, but Rhodesia is winning through, because no one there trusts the U.K. and they know that they can save Rhodesia for the civilised world. I went there in 1962 and what I heard from great leaders like Roy Welensky left me in no doubt that in their heart of hearts none of them trust those at Westminster, except such as Stephen Hastings, Patrick Wall and now Julian Amery, just returned to the Commons in my place. They do not forget that, whilst we were losing out in Tanzania, Kenya etc. Alec Douglas-Home, Duncan Sandys, Reggie Maudling and Iain Macleod were all in turn in charge of their affairs. They still feel that for these men other things come before Rhodesia's problems; and whatever fine sentiments those, who are to be once again the Conservative leaders of tomorrow, preach today, who can trust that they will not find an excuse on return to power to pacify instead the United Nations?

No, from what I have seen there and in Angola and Mozambique, there seems to me no honourable alternative, but to let the people whose whole stake is in the centre of Africa have their own way and see if they cannot develop a far happier African world than any we can offer them. Next to Rhodesia are the Portuguese territories—would that they were richer, so that they could go ahead more quickly. Brazil, once a Portuguese Colony, is slowly moving towards joining Portugal in developing her African overseas provinces—this may be yet another African solution and indeed a South American one as well. But don't let anyone say : "Portugal has held these lands for 300 years—what have they made of them?" The answer is that the modern inventions which are making South Africa and other parts of the world so successful today did not exist even fifty years ago and Portugal, with what money she possesses, is doing what she can today and very successfully.

She does not believe in some of the teachings of South Africa and she will not give up her way of life which certainly makes Angolans and others very happy. Luckily we have at Westminster people like John Biggs-Davison and others who have visited these parts of the world. Would that not only the Labour Party but many Conservative leaders would listen to them—not that it matters because we have lost our influences there !

Having tried in pre-war and early post-war years to study these problems and having hoped that our leaders would then go ahead constructively, I have indeed felt frustration as I have seen our post-war policies develop. One ex-Colonial Secretary told me that he felt, since we decided to educate the native to try and make him a Christian and as good as ourselves, and then advocated one man one vote, and as we had no money to enforce anything anyway, the best thing to do was to get out of our Colonies as quickly as we could and with what dignity we could. To which I replied : "But if chaos ensues, after the promises we have made to our own settlers there?" He just shrugged his shoulders. I cannot be carried away by these men's speeches now and I don't believe White Rhodesians can either, or even our European allies.

Macmillan may have been correct that the wind of change had come—but if we are not prepared to stand up to it, then why not be honest and let our own kith and kin look after themselves and not tie one of their arms behind them? And why can we not recognise that the average African is not Socialist enough to despise his Chieftain? The history of these areas has developed on tribalism and I do not believe the areas want anything else, even though Red China and possibly Russia have tried to filter in an unwanted Communism.

I was especially struck by this when I went to see Moise Tshombe in 1962 in Katanga. Every effort was made to stop my going there by, to my amazement, an old friend of mine who I would have thought would have helped me—Lord Alport, the British High Commissioner in Salisbury. But Sir Roy Welensky saw to it that I got to Elizabethville. It was at moments frightening and it was not easy, the town was all in ruins and in the concentration camps on the town's edge, people were openly being killed and eaten by each other at the rate of a dozen or so a day. Lord Russell of Liverpool was also there: the Americans thought that he was Bertrand Russell and could not understand what sort of passive protest he was trying to organise. I had two long talks with Tshombe. He told me about the tribal links of the area as well as with neighbouring Angola. How right was Roy Welensky in telling me that he thought Tshombe was the most intelligent African he had ever met!

Tshombe was very bitter about the Americans and the way that they were fighting quite unscrupulously for economic control of the Congo. He said that he owed his life to a Motion Tony Fell and several others of our group, including myself, had put down on the Order Paper of the House of Commons, just before he was about to be bumped off in prison—which goes to show that perhaps British back-benchers have sometimes more influence than they realise. Later he sprang into power again and, thanks to Lord Russell of Liverpool and Lord Colyton, he came to London for a few days, spoke in a Commons Committee Room and was given a big dinner at the Savoy.

*   *   *

Perhaps the organisation doing most for civilisation is located in the Iberian Peninsula. Its object is to uphold Christian prin-

15.   The Author and the present Regent of Greece, 1969.

16. A memo of the Author's visit to Guyana. The first Speaker of the Guyana Parliament and the Governor General, 1966.

ciples internationally, and especially in Europe generally. It is an
organisation called the C.E.D.I. (Centre Européen de Documen-
tation et Information). It was first started in the early fifties after
a Eucharistic Congress in Barcelona. Spain then felt very "out
of" European thought and was not encouraged to join the European Movement. The Archduke Otto, Pretender to the Austrian
and Hungarian thrones, was approached by Franco to organise
something on rather more religious lines than what was building
up at Strasburg. One of the first meetings was at the Escorial,
near Madrid in 1952. Walter Starkie, the head of the British
Council, and myself, both Catholics, were the first two members
to represent the U.K. The Spaniards could not understand this,
since we were both Southern Irish and came from the Republic
of Ireland—but it worked and I am still a member. Bit by bit the
organisation grew. The Germans (then led by the Deputy Speaker
of the Bundestag), France, represented by the equivalent of our
Lord Chancellor, Belgium, Sweden, Austria, the Vatican, Portugal, Liechtenstein, Italy, Greece and Turkey now all belong and I
believe that there are over 100 members, people with influence
either in Government, Diplomacy or the Press, or prominent landowners and ex-Royalty. The meetings are usually in Madrid or
Paris or Portugal or Rome and, even once, we met in London
when Geoffrey Rippon, who runs the U.K. branch called the
March Club with Sir James Greenwood, a great local government
expert, organised it superbly with Sir Denys Lowson, giving a
wonderful banquet still talked about abroad.

A new Chairman takes over every three years and the last one
was Sir John Rodgers, M.P. for Sevenoaks, who is also in charge
of J. Walter Thompson & Co. in London. He was given special
Spanish decorations and was succeeded by a well-known former
Portuguese Colonial Minister who I remember well, con-
trolled my visit to Angola in 1962—not a very easy time, as
Portugal had the week before lost Goa and laid the blame on us.
Fearing that something might happen to me, our Ambassador,
Archie Ross, came down to the Airport with me at midnight to
make sure that all was well. But it was not so well when I reached
Luanda. There to welcome me the Governor had ordered two
minutes' silence, one for Goa and one for "False friends". In the

N

end all was forgiven and I saw an awful lot of what the terrorists were doing and had done. The C.E.D.I. is a most useful international Conservative organisation, going from strength to strength and needs more Conservative British M.P.s as members.

*   *   *

Since we have been in Opposition, especially since Wilson's major victory in 1966, I have realised, from Conservative friends abroad, how little now we count internationally. But it is not only us. Over the last six years the world has been jumping ahead as never before and inventions have developed so fast they have left way behind the well-tried nineteenth-century and early twentieth-century methods of Government. But not everybody realises it.

Who, since 1966, are the Members of the House of Commons? The majority are Socialists officially. They are rewarded retired Trade Union officials or some more active ones. They are young teachers and even a few professors, but they know terribly little about nuclear weapons, few are technocrats, a few—especially the older ones—know anything much about the inventions of the last ten years or even about finance. The standard of intelligence of M.P.s has definitely deteriorated over the years. They let millions of money be voted without a debate—all that is left to the civil servants.

One result is that, since the Socialists came to power, we are over £3,000 millions more in debt and the Conservatives will be expected to try to pay that off before they can "make a new world". We know we are bankrupt, but we think that no one else knows it. We forget the inventions which bring transistors and the like to backward people in the heart of Africa—or China—who just laugh at Wilson's boasts when they hear the facts about the latest efforts for us to get loans.

Now new inventions make it possible to see what is going on the other side of a walled-in room. There is no longer any privacy. It might interest M.P.s to know that only recently an ex-Minister told me of what he knew for certain when he was a Minister; namely that every M.P.s private telephone is tapped whenever the powers that be feel like it. Not your office 'phone, but the one in your own home. If my friend wants to make a private call, even now, he never makes it from his home.

These are things which even Hitler never could do. In Russia and in China they are now every day matters. Elections may come and go, but they won't make much difference soon. I think our Government realises this and wants to rid itself of as much outside responsibilities as possible.

In 1965 I went through the Caribbean area by myself and to Guyana with William Whitlock. There was already a growing Colour resentment towards the British. We had over the years taken a lot away from the West Indies and given them but little in return. Enoch Powell had not yet started his immigration campaigns. Since then things have got much worse and will no doubt get worse still. The race question has certainly blown up under socialism and must be a terrible thorn in Heath's side, but it does not worry the rest of the world and nobody appreciates this problem of ours.

Abroad, people seem more to be taking up positions over Russia, China and the U.S.A. and do not see the U.K. in this pattern. We have no money, and no troops worth talking about; we only have know-how and that is not necessarily in Parliament. Today we hear that the U.S.A. wants to make friends with China so as to be able to embarrass the U.S.S.R., hence also her sudden interest in Roumania. The U.S.A. would also like Western Germany to set up again her many claims against the U.S.S.R., whilst the U.S.S.R. looks West for allies and also East to behind China and to Nationalist China and Japan. We have steadily tried to keep ourselves outside this pattern and we quarrel instead over the House of Lords, over Education and over morals.

Luckily there is still a fine intake in the Conservative Party—steadily moving to the Right—and don't let us forget good ex-M.P.s, who still nurse ungrudgingly their former seats. They should get back and deserve jobs. To name but two, Sir Richard Thompson and Dame Pat Hornsby-Smith who have been loyal to their supporters.

I think that I can see its leaders of the day-after-tomorrow—Rippon, Amery, Balniel, Ridley, Eldon Griffiths are all good for fifteen years—but we will have to let our present team play themselves out. The Monday Club, Right Clubs and many travellers to sympathetic foreign countries need every encouragement, so that they can get the approach other countries are making to face up to the revolutionary world changes that are going on. We have a mass of dining Clubs in the Commons, but how many of them put first things first; very few I fear and now, until this Parliament is over, I can see little being done to alter anything except accommodation. And is that necessary? What does it obtain for M.P.s? A new room to themselves for each and every one. Will that help us?

The best club in London is nearly finished and we will be back to those days in wartime I described earlier on in this book when M.P.s met but rarely and only came to Westminster to vote. Government went on without them—so will it again, with Civil Servants in control—but they may be international ones in Brussels or in Zurich.

CHAPTER XVII

NEARING THE END OF 25 YEARS

LOOKING BACK I would say that two remarks in Parliament have given me the key to most of our frustrations.

The first was at a dinner the Conservative Chief Whip used to give every so often to chosen groups of M.P.s to discuss our problems. It was in the days when we had a big majority. One M.P. asked: "But why don't we do something really constructive?" to which he replied: "We are too big a Party in power; we are not just a Conservative Party, but a national party; there are too many different opinions in the Party; and my job is to see that we all keep together and that the Party does not split; so nothing too controversial."

The other remark was on the Floor of the House when Labour was in power and Herbert Morrison was Leader of the House. He said that the rules of the House were made for gentlemen and meant to be kept by gentlemen. If this was not done, we might as well pack up as chaos would develop—there must be plenty of give and take.

Of course chaos did develop when Parnell and his Home Rule followers broke the gentlemen's agreements in the last century. But bit by bit both the Liberals and the Tories wore him down. It is not so now. We live in a period when few believe our chaotic old time agreements can work any longer. The whole system is hopelessly out of date, and so, I think, believe the majority of the country. We have foisted our democracy on endless colonies and one by one they are throwing our system overboard. But there seems no one big enough in Parliament to sweep our cobwebs away. Judging by the present Parliament and those who are likely to be in the next one, we are unlikely to solve our problems even then. Should there be a big majority for one side or the other, we will just drift on; and should there be only a small majority, then no one will dare risk adventures.

Churchill's 1951 Government will, I think, one day when the facts can be published, be looked on as a major disaster. He might have altered much. Europe had hopes in him, but when he got back to power he forgot, it would seem, all about his dreams and his ideals. Admittedly he had but a small majority, and he had inherited an almighty mess—but he was too old a man to give us a lead. Eden's administration was short-lived, shook our American links and divided the country. When he went, Selwyn Lloyd should have gone as well—but he remained to go to the Treasury and finally be ruthlessly dismissed from there, leaving us as a legacy the Capital Gains Tax which even Stafford Cripps refused to risk. A very lovable man, and one of Churchill's brigadiers, he has now drifted into a sort of Elder Statesman—but I doubt if he will ever do much to solve Parliament's problems.

The arrival of Macmillan as Leader when we seemed most in despair after Suez was the sort of stroke of luck the Conservative Party sometimes gets, but does not always deserve. I was in Italy when Eden resigned, but I had left my proxy for Macmillan. He first pulled his Party together in the House, then in the country, and finally won his massive victory of 1959.

Why then did we not go on to far greater heights? The answer, I feel, lies in the Chief Whip's comment I mentioned earlier in this chapter.

Slowly but surely also, scandals were developing at home and the African problem was disillusioning many of us. At that time we had several State visits from South American Presidents. I happened to be invited to many of the functions. Macmillan, seeing me at them, presumably thought that I knew something about South America. He said to me : "But if the Spaniards and the Portuguese were able to blend with the natives and still remain the ruling class once they had broken away from Europe— is there not hope that over a period we may be able to develop such a solution for Africa?" His mind was evidently thinking along those lines then, but I respectfully reminded him that we now had transistors, films and telegraphic news all over Africa. We had not the time in Africa, Europeans had had in South America. Rhodesia and South Africa may, I hope, prove me wrong.

Other great problems facing an already tired Macmillan (for these days to be a Prime Minister for a long time is a strain only Wilson seems to be able to bear) were those of the Common Market and especially De Gaulle and Eisenhower. When the Summit met in Paris—it will be remembered that, as luck would have it, an American photographic aircraft was shot down by the U.S.S.R.—it broke up the Summit. All De Gaulle said to Macmillan when he heard the news was *"tant pis"* and shrugged his shoulders; but poor Eisenhower was desperately depressed and Macmillan thought he seemed so lonely that he took him for a long motor drive round Paris.

On another occasion De Gaulle thought that he would be kind to Macmillan. When he came to England he said that he did not want to stay at Chequers; he would prefer to stay at Macmillan's private home, Birch Grove. It was meant to be a friendly gesture, but caused difficulties. There was not sufficient staff. Then the Foreign Office rang up and said that they were sending down a sample of the Presidential blood in case an attempt was made on his life. It was carried wherever he went and it must be kept in the refrigerator.

"Good gracious," said Macmillan, "I'd better go and ask the cook." He did and she was most emphatic that the 'frig was already full of fish. In the end it had to be laid out on the tennis court and covered in blocks of ice.

The night the President arrived he and Macmillan went into the library and were not to be disturbed. Suddenly there was a loud knock on the door. No answer. Then a louder one; Macmillan thought the house might be on fire. He opened it to find his gamekeeper.

"Sir," said the gamekeeper, "this must stop."

"What must stop?"

"All these detectives prowling around the woods with their dogs. Don't forget, Sir, you've got a shoot on Saturday and I won't guarantee there'll be any birds."

When Macmillan went back to De Gaulle the latter just continued saying : *"Quand nous étions interrompus...."*

But undoubtedly what hurt the Conservative Party most in those last few years of power was the Common Market; De Gaulle's determination that we should not come in and swamp his leadership; Heath's almost fanatical efforts to get in; and the very strong feeling of so many of us that it would be our ruination. I remember discussing it with Michel Debré, the French Premier. He rightly pointed out that we had had our chance of leadership when Churchill came back to power in 1951, but he let the whole thing slide.

There is a very interesting Dining Club which meets in London, it is full of British diplomats, bankers, businessmen, a few M.P.s, members of the Queen's Court and coming young military men. On one occasion Sir Derek Walker-Smith, who is our leading anti-Common Market M.P.; and on another Edward Heath spoke. I took the Chair on both occasions. I noticed that Heath was so detailed in his knowledge of facts that he quite floored the doubting bankers and businessmen. They were impressed, but I don't think convinced. Anyway, Heath so pushed for the Common Market that it looked as if people like myself would have to stand down at the next General Election. He wanted no compromise. De Gaulle, of course, saved us and thus left us without any policy to fall back on, and now Derek Walker-Smith and the group I belonged to in the Commons look as if we may be proved completely right, especially as regards the cost of living. Perhaps Wilson will go into battle for the Common Market—if he does, Heath will have lost yet another plank for his Election programme, but it may save us as a Party.

When De Gaulle, however, flatly turned us down, we seemed politically left with no policy. We had been seldom consulted in Committee and I refused to go to the Blackpool Conference in 1963 having felt sufficiently humiliated at the Llandudno one, when all my local representatives were wildly pro-Common Market.

The next few days after the Blackpool Conference are now well-known and Macmillan, having resigned, refused a peerage because I think that he thought within a year he would be well again and, if Alec Douglas-Home did not win the Election, it might be necessary to recall him again. For a long time it looked as if this might well be so.

The superb effort made by Sir Alec is now history. I offered to resign my seat for him but he told me he wanted a Scottish seat. Central Office made the bad mistake of running him too hard on the television and in the country. Had they left him alone he could be our Prime Minister today—unless of course the intrigues that developed after the election had arisen anyway. It is well that we should not forget that these intrigues have left their mark and that all this began to happen less then five years ago.

Our defeat in 1964 was so slight and the period Sir Alec Douglas-Home had had as Prime Minister so short, that to my mind it was a great triumph for Home. There had, however, been serious critics of how he had been elected Leader of our Party and had therefore become Prime Minister, and no doubt they told in the elections. Be that as it may, Home immediately decided to alter the method for choosing a leader; but it was to be after he had retired. He announced to us his plan and we accepted it.

Then the intrigues began. Wilson watched from across the Benches with amusement. After all, he was in with a tiny majority and so no one on his side would try to make things difficult for him, and in addition he had rushed through a measure—previously agreed by the Parties—which gave us greatly increased pay, though even then hardly enough, and a pension scheme which meant that older Members with longer than ten years' service did not get any extra benefits and which seemed to me, for the future, to be so designed that long service in the House would not be greatly encouraged.

I went to a Conference in the Far East where I was asked to comment on the results of the Elections and I mentioned that this new pay increase would mean greater power for a leader, since M.P.s would not want to give the pay up lightly. A German Press reporter got a copy of what I said and sent a garbled version back to London. There was a move in the Labour Party to have me censured for breach of parliamentary privilege—but it came to nothing.

Home in his new code for leadership election laid it down that whoever eventually got elected should have the full support of the Party. But the election no longer included Peers nor the Party Executive; it was merely a House of Commons affair.

It was not long before the intrigues became such that Alec, who had sacrificed so much for the Nation and the Party and never wanted power for power's sake, got disgusted and decided to throw his hand in. It happened suddenly at a 1922 Committee meeting. As always when something important is about to happen the whisper had got around and the room was packed. Alec was nearly in tears. Many of us were nonplussed. Greville Howard spoke up manfully and begged him not to go—but he was determined. Later he wrote to me in a little different tone saying "he hoped that he had made the right decision". Previously he had felt certain.

Three candidates put up for the Leadership—Heath, Maudling and Powell. Had Powell not stood, I am not sure that Maudling would not have won. Some of those rooting for Heath lost their seats at the next election—but they have mostly found their way back to support him.

Some people, I do not know who, put out a rumour on the Monday before the election that Maudling was an atheist and it looked as if this well might do him great harm. I was definitely a Maudling man and had known him since we worked together at the Air Ministry during the war. I rang him up and asked him if he would give me authority to deny this. He replied: "Of course," and added a little bitterly: "My wife and I went to Church on Sunday here in Chester Square. It's funny that nobody bothered to find out and that all the photographers were at the Church to which Heath went!" In the end Heath won, but it is forgotten by how small a majority.

According to the rules of the game Reggie Maudling had the right to try a second time. I begged him so to do, but he would not. Heath had won; Heath should now be followed and he has kept his word ever since. Alec Home has also followed in blind loyalty as far as we can see; and it has been said that, only if Heath were himself to come and ask him to take back the leadership, would he consider such a thing. But Heath is quite determined to stay.

A friend of mine, a newspaper owner, a year or two ago was asked by Heath to come and see him at Albany.

Said Heath : "Why do you not like and support X ?" to which my frank friend replied : "Because he's so like you."

Heath replied : "I've no intention of being pushed out."

He, like Wilson, is determined at all costs to be the boss, which in a way is a good thing; a strong leadership is needed everywhere these days.

CHAPTER XVIII

THE FUTURE

THE DAY Heath was elected to the Tory Party leadership I ran into Lord Wigg. "You may think that he will be better able to stand up to Wilson in Opposition than Alec Home, but if he ever becomes Prime Minister he will be a very bad one," was his comment. Will he be Prime Minister and, if so, for how long? And what team will he have to work with him and what sort of a Party will he have behind him?

To start with the last question first. There will be those who are already in the House and they will be far younger than the present Opposition. Those who were in Parliament before 1936 will have nearly all gone. Charles Taylor will be Father of the House and he got in in 1935. A large number of those who got in before 1951 will also have gone and their successors will be mostly ex-M.P.s who, on balance, are about 50/50 Radical or Right Wing. With the exception of Christopher Chataway (on the Left) and Julian Amery (to appease the Right Wing—though Julian is not so very Right Wing on Home Affairs), none are likely to be given office.

Wilson has stolen a march on Heath once again and has cut down the size of his Cabinet. Since we must know already who will be in the Cabinet, in this book there is no point in my discussing them, since they are so well-known, but two deserve to be mentioned; Robert Carr, in case he becomes Minister of Labour, and Lord Balneil—who has been doing so well in various "Shadow" jobs that Heath may have doubts about taking him on, as Heath will not tolerate being over-shadowed.

Labour problems must be our chief worry; is Carr likely to be able to overcome them? This was the question Labour always asked when Churchill came back in 1951—but Churchill suddenly chose out of the blue Walter Monckton who even Labour could not resent since he had never really been a politician or committed to any one policy. He was successful, but largely because Churchill told him to give way on almost every point—a policy of appeasement.

Carr is, however, a businessman without any very glamorous personality; a former P.P.S. of Eden's and, if we are to believe Heath's statements, there will be but little appeasement of Trade Unions. We can then look for open warfare if the Conservatives are returned. A grim prospect when we remember the state of the nation's economy. Unless, of course, Heath springs another surprise by making Enoch Powell his Minister of Labour!

But, to be serious, what is the future for Enoch Powell and will he ruin the Conservative Party? Britain has, as long as I can remember, had such political problem children. There were Lloyd George, Churchill, Nye Bevan and now Michael Foot and Enoch Powell. The first two were wonderful in wartime. Many people say that Nye Bevan lost Labour a million votes when at one Election he came out with a suggestion that whatever the election results meant in return of M.P.s, if there were more votes for Labour (and there were), Labour would go on ruling regardless. This is a possibility that we may yet one day see come to pass—but not quite yet.

Enoch Powell can certainly lose us a million votes, or I suppose he would argue that if Heath will not withdraw then it is Heath who will lose us a million votes. But what is behind Powell's moves? I can only guess, as others who see just a little of him guess. He is, like Churchill was, convinced that he is necessary to the country. Yet what has he ever done politically and how has he done it? He was at the Treasury and went with the Chancellor, Thorneycroft, when the latter felt that we were taking on internationally more than we could afford; we still are doing this, especially in our Conservative promises. Powell then, I believe, stated that he would never take office again unless he was in actual charge of a Department. He was made Minister of Health. The medical journals of the day say that what he told us all was completely wrong. He denied that doctors were leaving the country or would do so in increasing numbers. He was presumably completely in the hands of his Civil Servants who told him this. It has not only been proved wildly wrong, but it left the door open to much of the coloured migration which he now so deeply deplores. He would not take any advice from those doctors who were already in the House and who knew what they were talking about—but then that is probably our greatest weakness in the traditions of our Government.

In the Foreign Service or the Colonial Service, you would have thought that when someone comes back from some years in an area he would be posted in London to the same Department of his Ministry. Not a bit of it—he must go to deal with a country about which he knows nothing—the theory being that the new man must be given a free hand. Equally, when a benevolent Treasury allows some of the M.P.s to go on a visit to a Foreign or Commonwealth country you would think we would send those who know something about the country already. No, it must be someone who knows nothing about the area so that he, or they, may learn something however ephemeral about it. The same applies in the House. We have had several doctors there who knew about the National Health Service at first hand, such as Dr. Johnson, M.P. for Carlisle—but Powell would never listen; he only did what his Civil Servants told him. I pity poor Dr. Trafford when he gets in for The Wrekin, a brilliant specialist, he has already in Brighton had such passages of arms with a Labour Minister of Health that even the local Labour M.P., Dennis Hobden, felt he must publically apologise for the behaviour of his own Minister.

In more recent days, of course, we had Enoch Powell standing for election as Party Leader. He came well at the bottom of the poll, but his intervention I believe prevented Maudling from being elected our Leader and gave us Heath.

Thereafter he moved to immigration. He knew the form as well as anybody and that Quintin Hogg would be making the official speech on our side on this subject. When he had made his own speech first, without warning Hogg, Hogg, rightly I believe, said: "Either Powell leaves the Shadow Cabinet or I do."

As I used to see him sitting in his usual seat at a writing table in the Commons Library (he never comes into the Smoking Room) he has always looked to me worried and a little wild. His ear is certainly to the ground, he finds out better than Central Office what the country is feeling and then strikes. He is very clever, but he does not lead, he follows public opinion and then, irrespective of Party loyalty, snatches the leadership of the particular movement of the moment. This will not lead him to be Premier— at least I hope not—but it can easily lead him to splitting the Conservative Party so that we lose the election. He again is no Conservative; he is a dyed-in-the-wool Whig. For me, however, he is an encouragement since he senses the unpopularity of the Common Market and that to my mind could greatly affect the Tories at the coming election.

How far would that matter? There are, as I see it, three alternatives; a sweeping Tory victory, a tiny Tory majority or a tiny Labour majority. A sweeping Tory majority could be a good thing economically if we can avoid too many strikes (which I doubt) and would give confidence abroad in certain areas—but we would have as leaders people young enough to last for ages, but not impressive enough as to what they can do, or our Leader would allow them to do. A tiny majority would to my mind be disastrous. We would inherit an empty cupboard and we would not be strong enough to put through really drastic measures, whilst those elected to support our Government would be deeply divided as to the right remedies. After a short and not very fruitful period we would be swept away by Wilson, refreshed after a short spell in Opposition and full of "I told you so" criticisms, and Wilson would still be young enough to lead for another five to ten years. This is a very frightening thought.

But we have several really first-class Tories about to come to the fore. They are not yet known nationally and it will take two or three years before they are. I would put first Geoffrey Rippon, now our Shadow Minister for Defence, openly a member of the go-ahead Monday Club, a fearless Tory, brilliantly knowledgeable on Local Government, as well as Continental Local Government and an all-round leader. Not far behind him comes Julian Amery who could take the place of Duncan Sandys, now a little bit beyond his prime, but still a gallant fighter. There would be Nicholas Ridley, quiet but very effective; Angus Maude who cannot get on with Heath, and then a man who may yet be the leader of the lot, Eldon Griffiths. Eldon has great personality, speaks and writes well and is probably the most intelligent of the younger M.P.s being just over forty. He worked for Macmillans, the publishers, in America and wrote some of Alec Home's best speeches. He is right up to date on the American mind as well as the European, has a charming German wife and advises our Police Force, and if he does not get high office at once will be wasted by the frustrations of our system, for the country.

All this is why I cannot see that a tiny, and it must be tiny, Socialist majority at the next election would not in the long run be best for this country and for our Party. It could happen largely because of Powell's activities, especially as he becomes more popular in the Conservative Party, but also largely because of Ireland. There is little doubt that Callaghan has won great favour over what he has done about Northern Ireland as Home Secretary. Things may well not be settled by the time of the Election, but he has grasped the nettle. Remember there are both Catholic-Irish and Orangemen, all over England and Scotland and some of the loudest shouters in the Commons on Ulster are at most second or third generation Irish—or not even that— just M.P.s for areas with large Irish votes. Alas, the Conservatives have done themselves harm here by two people, however sincere and brilliant, but each one disliking the other. Enoch Powell by telling the Irish to get out, as if they were coloured, and Hogg by attacking the Irish national anthem and by alienating the Ulster Members at Westminster by his Brighton speech, brilliant though it was.

At the last Party Conference there were criticisms about how the leaders of the Party Organisation were elected, especially from the Young Conservatives. Should we be slightly defeated at the next election this would give time for reforms here to be initiated and no doubt it would also give the Party a chance to change again the method of electing our Leader. The muddle over Alec Home's election was followed by his own deciding how the new election of a Leader should take place. I personally have always felt that it was wrong that only the Conservatives in the Commons should choose the Leader. It runs the danger that the Party in the House may not always agree with the Party in the country and also the Peers were left out. If and when a new Leader is elected, and presumably if we were defeated at the next Election this would have to happen, then I feel that the National Union (itself reformed and not controlled by a Central Office completely in the power of the Party Leader) the Peers and the M.P.s and Candidates should do the electing. If Heath is re-elected, well and good; it is the Party wish and not just that of a small majority of Tory M.P.s and fresh air will have been let in to clear the Corridors of Frustration.

History never repeats itself, but often it nearly does. The position to my mind is very similar to the end of Attlee's first administration, except that Wilson is a much cleverer man than was Attlee.

It seemed to us certain that we would win in 1950—we had Churchill to lead us—he had done better than the Prime Minister in Opposition with his speeches abroad and his European Movement taking the limelight. We still were heavily rationed; my "surgery" was full every Saturday morning with people wanting advice as to how to fill up forms, and others showing me most embarrassingly their swollen legs and other reasons why they must have a National Health doctor, or a butcher nearer their homes. The young, who previously had expected everything, as in the war, to be done for them, were now getting restless and longing to do things on their own. It seemed impossible, as it seems in 1969 and 1970, that we could lose. But we did. Admittedly Attlee was only in by a very small majority and we had our new intake of brilliant backroom boys who were soon to rule the country for thirteen years with the help of a few leaders at the top; but it was very dispiriting. We had seemed so cock a'hoop, as we do today. It's a lesson we should learn and Churchill had become a great draw, greater than Heath.

The following year, 1951, Attlee decided to let us take over the wreck of the administration (which is what may happen to us yet in 1970 or after) and make what we could out of the mess. We succeeded, but many years were wasted. Eden, though not Prime

o

Minister until 1955, was already sickening—perhaps more than he realised—and the strain of being the "heir apparent" must have been awful. Once he lost his temper with me so violently that everyone was amazed. It was over a dinner Ernest Bevin was giving to a French Parliamentary Delegation and to which Eden had not been invited, but I had. Next day he came and charmingly apologized to me, adding: "Winston had been particularly difficult last evening."

Eden realised how necessary it now was to get into Parliament on our side more working class types and Heath I think realises it today—but it was hopeless and perhaps still is. A few have trickled in but they have made no real impact in the House and in most constituencies they are only just tolerated. I must make one notable exception, Ray Mawby, but even he with all his kindness, came up against the almost open hostility of the worker in the Socialist ranks and I think has never been able to break it.

Heath, of course, is himself of working class origin, but he has not had a working class life. A scholar at Oxford, he was only twenty-three when war broke out and he served right through it. He entered the House in February 1950 and was already a Whip by February the following year. From then on he steadily went ahead in the Whip's Office, becoming Deputy Chief Whip in July 1953 and Chief Whip in December 1955. His life, therefore, as a back-bencher has been practically nil and there was only one year, 1950/51, when he could make a speech (since Whips proverbially remain silent), until he went to the Ministry of Labour in October 1959 where he spoke hesitantly and was never a great success.

It is interesting today to remember that about that time he was very much against disturbing the *status quo* with the Trade Unions and when Capt. Kerby and Dr. Johnson put down a Motion to alter the Trade Union rules about strikes he was most anxious that they should take the Motion off. Similarly, later, a Motion by Sir John Rodgers—who after all had been at the Board of Trade—and many of his friends much worried him right up to the end of the 1959-64 Parliament. Rodgers was promised that legislation of a sort would be brought in in the next Parliament. But of course we had been turned out by then.

I was definitely against Heath taking over the leadership in July 1965 and both voted and "rooted" for Reggie Maudling. What now remains to be seen is how a man who has been for years a Chief Whip of the Party will make a good Prime Minister if we win. As far as I know there has never been one before, at any rate in my lifetime. Bobby Eyres-Monsell, Margesson, Patrick Buchan-Hepburn and Martin Redmayne have never done anything striking politically since each was Chief Whip. They have held Cabinet posts, yes, or been Governors-General, but never Party Leaders. James Stuart, who took so many of the knocks for Winston during the war and did so well as Secretary of State for Scotland later, was probably the most outstanding—but even he never aspired to leadership.

"Is the training suitable?" I ask myself. What has a Whip or Chief Whip to do? He has to know practically everything about every M.P. on his side of the House. Will that help him to take a detached view in choosing his Cabinet and his lesser Ministers? I notice he seems to rely mostly on young men who got in after he was head teacher. Unaccustomed to the rough and tumble of back-bench life, he has always looked with a rather jaundiced eye, as all Chief Whips must, on anyone who has shown initiative or rebellious instincts in the past.

I went through the days of Suez, first with Captain Charles Waterhouse, as one of his "Suez Rebels" Group in 1953/54. Heath was then Deputy Chief Whip and later we clashed again over the final fiasco of Suez when Eden, either because of ill health or bad advice, did not stand firm. From just before those days, it was Heath's job to advise the Cabinet what the Party would stand for and what it wanted. He was always friendly but distant. I remember later talking to a great friend of his who had been in the House, who told me that he always kept his thoughts to himself, he made no friends in the Commons except two, Dennis Vosper, M.P. for Runcorn, and Edward Wakefield, now both dead, and hardly ever confided even in them.

At first, Harold Macmillan thought a lot of him, perhaps not so much today, and Heath liked the atmosphere of a big country house. Is all this a little unfair? I hope not, but I cannot see how a Whip, and probably the best Whip we have ever had, who had started his career in the Whips' Office one year after getting into the House, can make a great leader. Let us hope that he will not be frustrated in governing the country by his experiences in Parliament.

INDEX

L

M

220 INDEX

Sèze, Vicomte de, 16
Segal, Lord, 187
Shakespeare, Geoffrey, M.P., 110
Sheridan, Clare, 106
Shawcross, Christopher, M.P., 152
Shawcross, Sir Hartley, M.P., 152
Shinwell, Emmanuel, M.P., 125, passim
Sikorski, General, 100, 101
Silverman, Sidney, M.P., 135
Silvertown, 12, 13, 32, 40
Simpson, Mrs. (Duchess of Windsor) 19, 56
Smith, Hon. James, 139
Smoot, Senator, 48
Snowden, Philip, M.P. (later Lord Snowden), 54
Southwood, Lord, 139
Spain, 193
Spears, Sir Edward, M.P., 152
Speyer, E. J. Mr., 177
Stalin, 116, et seq.
Stansgate, Lord, 72, 92
Stanley, Lady Maureen, 62, 68
Stanley, Oliver, M.P., 57, 96, 124, passim
Starkie, Walter, 193
Stewart, Peter, 37
Stewart-Brown, Nora, 37
Stokes, Richard, M.P., 94, 106, 110, 125, passim
Stonor, Sherman (later Lord Camoys), 167
Strachey, John, M.P., 19, 79
Straubenzee, William van, M.P., 161
Strickland, Miss Mabel, 163, 164, 168
Stuart, James, M.P., 76, 111, 190
Stuart, Lois, 34
Sueter, Admiral Sir Murray, 95
Summerskill, Dr. Edith, M.P., 69
Suez Canal Company, 153
Suez Rebels, 95

Sunday Express, 127
Swinton, 67
Sydney, 57

T

Taaffe, Mrs., 67
Tardini, Cardinal, 164
Taylor, Charles, M.P., 117, 146, 204
Tedder, Lord, 103
Teeling, Bartholemew, 14
Teeling, Charles, 91
Thesiger, Ernest, 34
Thesiger, Gerald, 22
Thomas, J. H., M.P., 54
Thomas, J. P. L., M.P., 31, 74, 96
Thomson, Lord, 180
Thompson, Richard, M.P., 195
Thomson, George, M.P., 179
Thorneycroft, Peter, M.P., 111, 121, 205
Throckmorton, Lady, 32
Thurtle, Ernest, M.P., 152
Times, The, 50, 51, 101, 181
Timoshenko, Marshal, 116
Tito, 103
Tone, Wolfe, 14
Topham, Mr. 182
Tory Reform Group, 111
Townsend, Group Captain, 136
Trafford, Dr., 206
Tredegar, Lord, 34
Tree, Ronald, M.P., 13
Tryon, Lord, 71
Tshombe, Moise, 192
Tucker, Miss Daisy, 35
Tucker, Ian, 139

U

United States of America, 57, et seq.
Universe, The, 157, 160